JASON MRAZ

CONTENTS

This book was approved by Jason Mraz

Cherry Lane Music Company
Director of Publications/Project Editor: Mark Phillips
Project Coordinator: Rebecca Skidmore

ISBN 978-1-60378-196-1

Visit our website at www.cherrylaneprint.com

You and I Both

Words and Music by
Jason Mraz

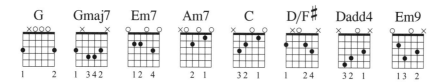

Verse 1

‖**G**
Oh, was it you   who spoke the words
        |**Gmaj7**
That things would happen, but not to me?
   |**Em7** |
Oh, things are gonna happen natural - ly.
   |**Am7** |
Oh, taking your advice and I'm looking on the bright side
   |**C** |**D/F♯**
And balancing the, the whole thing.

Verse 2

        ‖**G** |**Gmaj7**
Oh, but at often times those words, they get tangled up in a lines;
        |**Em7** |
And the bright lights turn to night,
        |**Am7**
Oh, un - til the dawn, it brings
   |**Am7** |**C** |**D/F♯**
An - other day to sing about the mag - ic that was you and me.

Chorus 1

```
          ‖G                    |Gmaj7
'Cause you and I   both loved
          |Em7                  |
What you and I      spoke of
          |Am7                  |
And others just      read of.
     |C                         |D/F♯
Others on - ly read of, of the love,
              |G                |Gmaj7
Of the love that I   love,       yeah.
              |Em7              |
La - ba - da - ba,       yeah.
```

Verse 3

```
                 ‖G
See, I'm all about them words
     |Gmaj7                        |Em7
Over num   -   bers, unencumbered numbered words,
     |Em7                |Am7
Hundreds of pages, pages, pages for - wards.
          |Am7
More words      than I had ever heard,
C                      |D/F♯
   And I   feel so alive.
```

Chorus 2

```
            ‖G                        |Gmaj7
'Cause you and I   both loved,
                        |Em7                   |
Uh, what you and I      spoke of
                   |Am7
And others just    read of.
                        |C              D/F♯          |
And if you could see  me now, oh,      love, love.
G                                      |
 You and I, you and I,
Gmaj7                          |Em7                    |
Not so little, you and I any - more,           mm.
        |Am7                            |
And a with this silence brings a moral story
                          |C                    |D/F♯
More importantly evolv - ing is the glory of a boy.
```

Chorus 3

```
            ‖G                        |Gmaj7
'Cause you and I   both loved,
                        |Em7                   |
Uh, what you and I      spoke of, of
                   |Am7
And others just    read of.
                        |C
And if you could see   me now,
                   D/F♯                |G
Well, then I'm almost finally out  of,
                   |Em7
I'm finally out        of,
                |Am7
Finally di  -  di - di - di - di - di.
                   |C              D/F♯              |G                        |
Well, I'm al - most finally, fi  -  nally, well, I    am free.    Oh, I'm free.
```

4

Bridge

         ||C   **|Dadd4**
And it's okay   if you had to go a - way.

            |G   **D/F♯**
Oh, just remem - ber that telephones,

                       |Em9
Well, they're workin' 'em both   ways.

        |C   **|Dadd4**
But if I   never ever hear them   ring,

            |G
If nothing else, I'll think the bells inside

         |Em7
Have finally found you someone else.

           |C   **|**
And that's   okay

           |Dadd4   **|**
'Cause I'll re - member everything you say.

Chorus 4

         ||G   **|Gmaj7**
'Cause you and I   both loved,

                |Em7   **|**
Uh, what you and I   spoke of, of

            |Am7
And others just   read of.

                |C
And if you could see   me now,

         D/F♯   **|G**
Well, then I'm almost finally out   of,

           |Em7   **|**
I'm finally out   of,

         |Am7
Finally di - di - di - di - di - di.

       |C   **D/F♯**   **|G**   **|**   **||**
Well, I'm al - most finally, fi - nally, well, out   of words.

5

I'll Do Anything

Words and Music by
Jason Mraz
Additional Words by
Billy Galewood

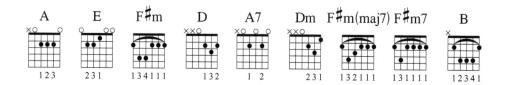

A   E   F#m   D   A7   Dm   F#m(maj7)   F#m7   B

Intro   A   E |F#m   D |A   E |F#m

Verse 1

‖A   E
Go make your next choice, be your best   choice.
|F#m   D
And if you're looking for a boy with a   voice,
            |A   E |F#m   D |
Well, baby, I'm   single.
A   E
Are you in the mood for some   dude?
            |F#m   D
Are you in the mood to be subdued,
                        |A   E |F#m   D
Or would you rather just   mingle?
            |A   E
Let's get   set then, to go   then,
            |F#m   D
Or let us jet set. We'll be like the Jetsons.
                        |A   E |F#m   D
You can be Jane,   my wife. Should I   marry Jane to - night?

Chorus 1

            ‖A
See, I would,
            |A7
If I could.
            |D |Dm
I'll do anything sponta - neously.

Verse 2

```
          ‖A                           E
Or we can keep chilling like ice cream filling.
          |F♯m                    D
We can be cool in the gang if you'd rather hang.
       |A              E        |F♯m              D
Ain't no thing. I can be la - cubrious with you.
       |A                E
I got no if, ands, ors, no wits or what's about it.
       |F♯m                             D                        |
But this place is getting crowded and my house is two blocks away,
A        E      |F♯m              D
   Or   maybe       closer.
```

Chorus 2

```
               ‖A
See, I would,
                 |A7
Oo, if I could.
               |D            |Dm
I'll do, oh, anything  sponta - neously.
                      |A
You know I would,
        |A7
Oh, if I     could.
               |D            |Dm                        ‖
I would do, oh, anything  sponta - neously.
```

Bridge

```
    F♯m                    |F♯m(maj7)
       If you could be nim      -      ble,
                |F♯m7              |B              |
You'd have it sim   -   ple just like me.
    F♯m                   |F♯m(maj7)
       So go on and try              it,
                |F♯m7              |B      |D      |Dm
Do not deny      yourself your free   -   dom.
```

7

Verse 3

              ||**A**   **E**
So step on up to the plate, get a date with Mraz.

          |**F♯m**   **D**
See, you better act fast because sup - plies, they never last.

             |**A**   **E** |**F♯m**   **D**
Now, did you know this is a limited time of - fer?

                |**A**   **E**
So go make your mind up before our time's up.

     |**F♯m**   **D** |**A**   **E**
So you better start winding it up because the party's al - most over.

                  |**F♯m**   **D**
And if you should know, girl,   it's a little bit lower now.

Chorus 3

             ||**A**
See, I would do,

          |**A7**
Oh, if I could do,

              |**D** |**Dm**
I would do, oh, anything sponta - neously.

           |**A**
You know I would,

          |**A7**
Oh, and I could prove it,

        |**D** |**Dm** ||
Oh, that I'll do anything sponta - neously.

The Remedy
(I Won't Worry)

Words and Music by
Graham Edwards, Scott Spock, Lauren Christy and Jason Mraz

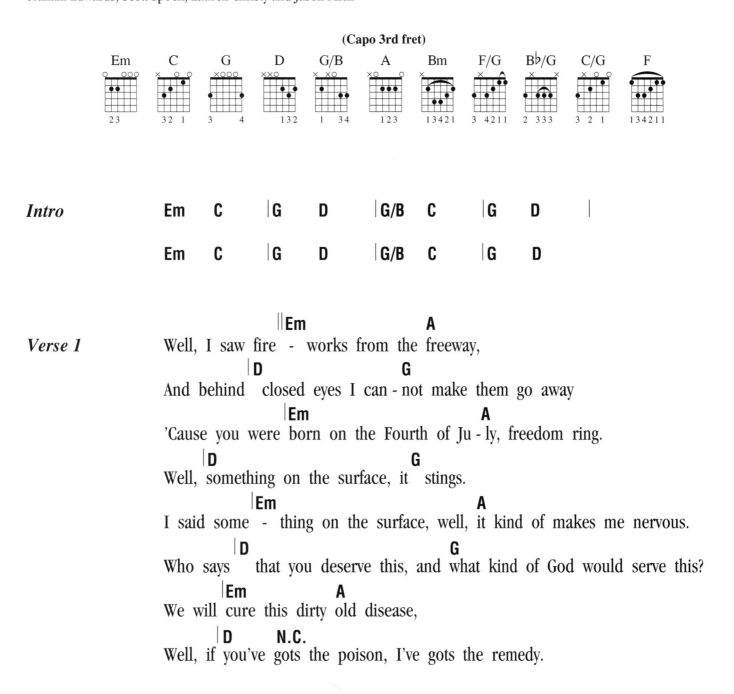

(Capo 3rd fret)

Intro

| Em   C | G   D | G/B   C | G   D | |
| Em   C | G   D | G/B   C | G   D |

Verse 1

‖Em   A
Well, I saw fire - works from the freeway,

|D   G
And behind   closed eyes I can - not make them go away

|Em   A
’Cause you were born on the Fourth of Ju - ly, freedom ring.

|D   G
Well, something on the surface, it   stings.

|Em   A
I said some - thing on the surface, well, it kind of makes me nervous.

|D   G
Who says   that you deserve this, and what kind of God would serve this?

|Em   A
We will cure this dirty old disease,

|D   N.C.
Well, if you’ve gots the poison, I’ve gots the remedy.

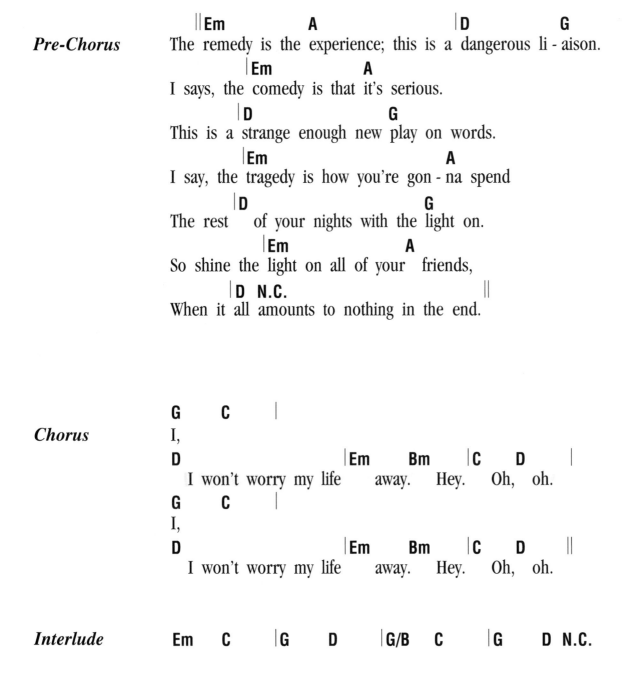

Pre-Chorus

```
  ‖Em              A                      |D           G
The remedy is the experience; this is a dangerous li - aison.
             |Em              A
I says, the comedy is that it's serious.
             |D              G
This is a strange enough new play on words.
             |Em                      A
I say, the tragedy is how you're gon - na spend
           |D              G
The rest    of your nights with the light on.
               |Em              A
So shine the light on all of your   friends,
           |D  N.C.                            ‖
When it all amounts to nothing in the end.
```

Chorus

```
  G      C        |
I,
D                           |Em      Bm  |C      D      |
  I won't worry my life    away.   Hey.  Oh,  oh.
G      C        |
I,
D                           |Em      Bm  |C      D      ‖
  I won't worry my life    away.   Hey.  Oh,  oh.
```

Interlude   Em   C |G   D |G/B   C |G   D N.C.

Verse 2

           ‖**Em**   **A**
Well, I heard two   men talking on the radio
         |**D**   **G**
In a cross - fire kind of new reality show.
       |**Em**   **A**
Un - covering the ways to plan the next big attack.
         |**D**   **G**
Well, they were counting down the ways to stab the brother in the...
        |**Em**   **A**
Be right back   after this, the un - avoidable kiss,
     |**D**   **G** |**Em**
Where the minty fresh death breath is sure to outlast this ca - tastrophe.
    A
Dance with me,
    |**D**   **N.C.**
'Cause if you've gots the poison, I've gots the remedy.

Repeat Pre-Chorus

Repeat Chorus

Bridge

Em |**C**
When I fall in love,   I take my time.
G |**D**
There's no need to hur - ry when I'm making up my mind.
Em |**C**
You can turn off the sun, but I'm still gonna shine,
G |**D**
And I'll tell you why.

Pre-Chorus 2

‖**G**   **C/G** |**F/G**   **B♭/G**
Because the remedy is the experience, this is a dangerous li - aison.
          |**G**   **C/G**
I says, the comedy is that it's serious.
          |**F/G**   **B♭/G**
This is a strange enough new play on words.
          |**G**   **C/G**
I say, the tragedy is how you're gon - na spend
          |**F/G**   **B♭/G**
The rest   of your nights with the light on.
          |**G**   **C/G**
So shine the light on all of your   friends,
          |**F   N.C.**   ‖
When it all amounts to nothing in the end.

Repeat Chorus

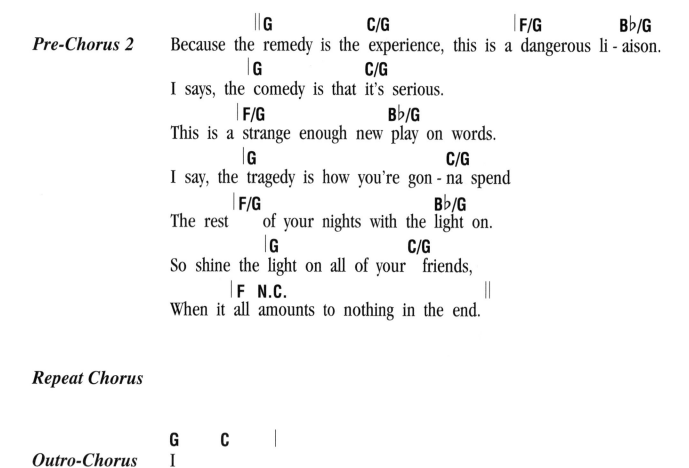

Outro-Chorus

G   **C** |
|
D |**Em**   **Bm** |**C**   **D** |
   I won't worry my life   away,   no.
G   **C** |
|
D |**Em**   **Bm** |**C**   **D** |**G**   ‖
   I won't worry my life   away.   Hey.   Oh,   oh.

Who Needs Shelter

Words and Music by
Jason Mraz, Chris Keup and Eric Shermerhorn

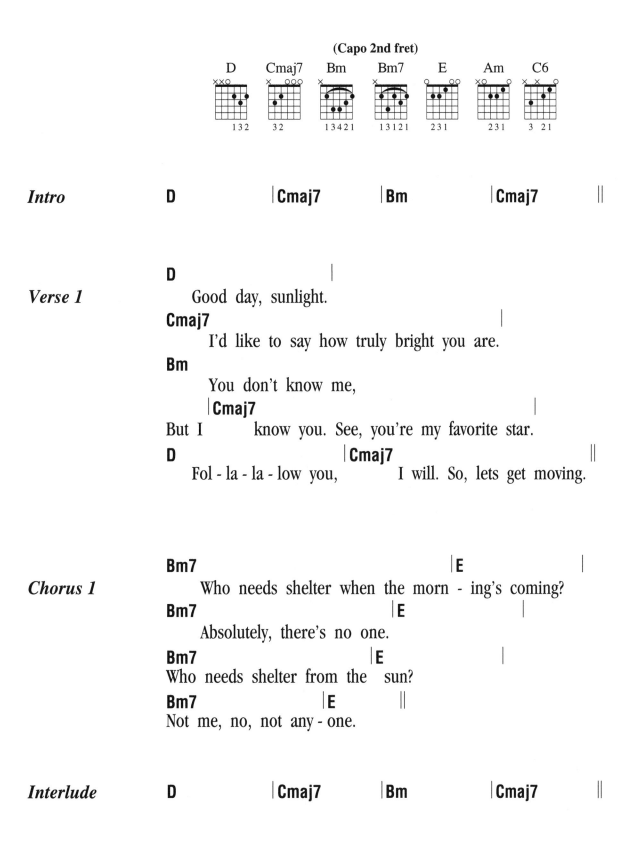

(Capo 2nd fret)

D   Cmaj7   Bm   Bm7   E   Am   C6

Intro   D |Cmaj7 |Bm |Cmaj7 ||

Verse 1

     D |
       Good day, sunlight.
Cmaj7 |
       I'd like to say how truly bright you are.
Bm
       You don't know me,
     |**Cmaj7** |
But I   know you. See, you're my favorite star.
D |**Cmaj7** ||
       Fol - la - la - low you,   I will. So, lets get moving.

Chorus 1

Bm7 |E |
       Who needs shelter when the morn - ing's coming?
Bm7 |E |
       Absolutely, there's no one.
Bm7 |E |
Who needs shelter from the   sun?
Bm7 |E ||
Not me, no, not any - one.

Interlude   D |Cmaj7 |Bm |Cmaj7 ||

Verse 2

```
        D
        By your clock the cock rooster crows,
        |Cmaj7                              |
Then  off  to  work  where  everybody  goes
Bm                                  |Cmaj7           |
        Slow, but eventually they get      there.
D
        They're picking up the day shift,
        |Cmaj7
Back         where all left off confined,
        |Bm
And      they're pecking at relationships.
        |Cmaj7                          ||Bm7
You  know,       it's only a worthless piece of shit.
```

Chorus 2

```
                                    |E                |
Who needs shelter when the morn - ing's coming?
Bm7                                |E              |
        Absolutely, there's no one.
Bm7                              |E                 |.
Who needs shelter from the  sun?
Bm7                        |E          ||
Not me, no, not any - one.
```

Bridge

```
Am              |E              |
        I'd sleep it all away,
Am                      |E              |
        But the sun won't let  me.
Am                  |E        |Em7      |              ||
        I'd miss those lovely days              of summer.
```

Interlude   **D** |**Cmaj7** |**Bm** |**Cmaj7** ||

D |

Verse 3   Well, good day, sunlight.

Cmaj7 |
      I'd like to say how truly bright you are.

Bm
      You don't know me,

   |**Cmaj7**   **C6** | ||
But I   know you. See, you're my favorite.

Curbside Prophet

Words and Music by
Jason Mraz, Billy Galewood and Christina Ruffalo

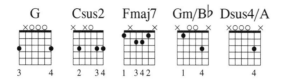

Intro   G   Csus2 |Fmaj7   Gm/B♭ Dsus4/A |

          G   Csus2 |Fmaj7   Gm/B♭ Dsus4/A

                  ‖G   Csus2

Chorus 1 I'm just a curbside prophet with my hand in my pocket,

              |Fmaj7   Gm/B♭ Dsus4/A

And I'm waiting for my rocket to come.

          |G   Csus2

I'm just a curbside prophet with my hand in my pocket,

              |Fmaj7   Gm/B♭ Dsus4/A   ‖

And I'm waiting for my rocket, y'all.   Hey.

Interlude G   Csus2 |Fmaj7   Gm/B♭ Dsus4/A |

               G   Csus2 |Fmaj7   Gm/B♭ Dsus4/A

Verse 1

```
             ‖G                         Csus2
You see, it started way back in NY  -  C
             |Fmaj7                    Gm/B♭  Dsus4/A
When I stole my first rhyme from the M-I-C
          |G                   Csus2
At-a West End Avenue at       Sixty-three.
                   |Fmaj7          Gm/B♭  Dsus4/A         |G
It's the be - ginning of a leap year, Februar - y,      ninety - six,
                         Csus2
When a guitar, picked it up in the mix.
           |Fmaj7                  Gm/B♭        Dsus4/A
I com - mitted to the licks a like a nickel bag of tricks.
          |G                  Csus2                |
Uh, well,    look at me now. Look at me now.
Fmaj7                        Gm/B♭      Dsus4/A
Look at me now, now, now,       now.
```

Repeat Chorus 1

Repeat Interlude

Verse 2

                   ‖G   **Csus2**
Well, then you'll never, da never, da guess what I bet,   bet, bet.

            |Fmaj7   **Gm/B♭**   **Dsus4/A**
And I have   no regrets that I bet   my whole check - ing account,

G   **Csus2**   **|Fmaj7**
  Because it all amounts   to nothing up in the end.

               Gm/B♭   **Dsus4/A**   **|G**
Well, you can only count   that "On the Road Again"

                   Csus2
Will soon be on my radio dial.

            |Fmaj7   **Gm/B♭**   **Dsus4/A**
And I been paying close attention to the Willie Nelson style.

       |G   **Csus2**
Like a,   a band of gypsies on the highway wild,

            |Fmaj7   **Gm/B♭**   **Dsus4/A** |
As I'm a one man mission on the California skyline.

G   **Csus2**
Drive up the coast and I brag and I boast

            |Fmaj7   **Gm/B♭**   **Dsus4/A** |
Because I'm picking up my pace. I'm makin' time like Space Ghost.

G   **Csus2**
Raising a toast to the high - way patrol at the most,

Fmaj7   **Gm/B♭**   **Dsus4/A**
     But my cruise control's   on coast

           |G   **Csus2**
'Cause I'm tour'n' around the nation on ex - tended vacation.

            |Fmaj7   **Gm/B♭**   **Dsus4/A**
See I got Elsa, the dog who exceeds   my limi - tation.

       |G   **Csus2**
I say, "I like your style, crazy pound pup.

            |Fmaj7   **Gm/B♭**   **Dsus4/A**
You need a ride? Well, come on, girl. Hop in the truck."

Chorus 2

```
         ‖G                          Csus2
With the curbside prophet with my hand in my pocket,
         |Fmaj7                      Gm/B♭  Dsus4/A
And I'm waiting for my rocket to come.
         |G                          Csus2
I'm just a curbside prophet with my hand in my pocket,
         |Fmaj7                      Gm/B♭  Dsus4/A
And I'm waiting for my rocket, y'all.
```

Repeat Chorus 2

Verse 3

```
         ‖G                          Csus2
See, I'm a down home brother, red - neck undercover
         |Fmaj7 N.C.
With my guitar here, I'm ready to play.
         |G                          Csus2        |Fmaj7 N.C.
And I'm a sucker for a filly, got a natural ability geared      to freestyle.
                                |
Look at my flexibility.
G                                   Csus2
Dangerous on the mic, my ghetto hat's cocked right.
         |Fmaj7 N.C.
All the ladies say, "Yo, that kid is crazy."
         |G                          Csus2
We got the backstage Betty's taking more than they can get.
         |Fmaj7 N.C.              Gm/B♭
They say,        "What's up with M-R-A-Z."
```

Outro

        Dsus4/A ‖**G**   **Csus2**
Uh, hey, hey, hey, hey. Uh, hey.

    |**Fmaj7**   **Gm/B♭**   **Dsus4/A**
Some - thing's different in my world today.

    |**G**   **Csus2** |**Fmaj7**   **Gm/B♭** **Dsus4/A**
Well, they changed my traffic   signs to a brighter yellow.

   |**G**   **Csus2**
Uh, hey, hey.

    |**Fmaj7**   **Gm/B♭**   **Dsus4/A**
Some - thing's different in my world today.

    |**G**   **Csus2** |**Fmaj7**   **Gm/B♭** **Dsus4/A**
Well, they changed my traffic   signs to a brighter yellow.

    |**G**   **Csus2**
I'm just a curbside proph - et, love,

  |**Fmaj7**   **Gm/B♭**   **Dsus4/A**
A curbside brother,   love,

  |**G**   **Csus2**
A curbside brother,   love,

  |**Fmaj7**   **Gm/B♭**   **Dsus4/A** |**G**   ‖
A curbside … Oh,   come on.

Sleep All Day

Words and Music by
Jason Mraz

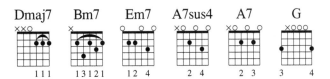

Intro

| Dmaj7 | |Bm7 | |Em7 | |A7sus4 A7 | |

Scat sing...

| Dmaj7 | |Bm7 | |Em7 | |A7sus4 A7 |

Verse 1

‖Dmaj7 |Bm7
Well, his after moan though cries, "Oh,   no."
    |Em7 |A7sus4   A7
He's building up a shine, but he take it   slow.
              |Dmaj7 |Bm7
And he knows it's time to make a change   here,
    |Em7 |A7sus4   A7
And time to get away.
                        |Dmaj7 |Bm7
And he knows it's   time for all the wrong reasons,
    |Em7 |A7sus4   A7
Oh, time to end the pain.

Chorus 1

‖Dmaj7 |
But he   sleep all, we sleep all day,
Bm7 |Em7 |A7sus4   A7
    Sleep all, we sleep all day   over.
              |Dmaj7 |
Why don't we,   sleep all, we sleep all day?
Bm7 |Em7 |A7sus4   A7
    Sleep all, we sleep all day   over.

Verse 2

  ‖Dmaj7   **|**

She said, uh,   "What would your mother think of all this?

Bm7

  How would your father react?

 |Em7   **|A7sus4**   **A7**

Oh,   would he take it all back, what they've   done?"

               |

"No way," they said.

Dmaj7   **|**

    Take it, take it." "He said,

Bm7   **|Em7**   **|**

  Make it with your own   two hands."

A7sus4   **A7**

  That was my old man, and he said,

 |Em7   **|**

"If   all is grounded, you should

G   **|Dmaj7**   **|**

  Go make a mountain out of it,   it."

Verse 3

  ‖Dmaj7   **|Bm7**

Oh, what a lovely day to have slice of humble pie.

    |Em7   **|A7sus4**   **A7**

Oh, re - calling of the while we used to drive and drive

                  |Dmaj7   **|Bm7**   **|Em7**

Here and there,   going no - where but for us.

                  |A7sus4   **A7**

Nowhere but the   two of us.

                  |Dmaj7   **|Bm7**

And we knew it was   time to take a chance   here,

 |Em7   **|A7sus4**   **A7**

And time to compromise our lives just   a little while.

         |Dmaj7   **|Bm7**

And it was time for all the wrong and lone - ly, lonesome reasons.

      |Em7   **|A7sus4**   **A7**

But time   is often on my side, but I give it to you tonight.

Chorus 2

‖**Dmaj7** |
And we   sleep all, we sleep all day,

Bm7 |**Em7** |**A7sus4**   **A7**
    Sleep all, we sleep all day   over.

                    |**Dmaj7** |
Why don't we,   sleep all, we sleep all day?

Bm7 |**Em7** |**A7sus4 A7**
    We sleep all, we sleep all day o - ver, and over, over and over a - gain.

Verse 4

                        ‖**Dmaj7** |
And, as the time   goes by, we get a little bit tired,

Bm7 |**Em7** |**A7sus4**   **A7**
Waking and baked another Marlboro mile   wide.

                        |**Dmaj7** |**Bm7**
It's sending the boys   on the run in the time in the hot summer sun

                        |**Em7**
To swim beneath, over, out - side.

                            |**A7sus4**   **A7**
Still they're reading between the lines.

            |**Dmaj7**
But they re - member the part in the Hallmark card,

        |**Bm7** |
Where they read about the dreams, and they're reaching for the stars

Em7 |**A7sus4**   **A7**
    To hold on a little bit closer to.

                    |**Dmaj7** |
Oo, they knew it was time, time to take, a take love,

Bm7 |
    Time to take a chance here,

Em7 |**A7sus4**   **A7**
Time to compromise, to occu   -   py the lives.

                    |**Dmaj7** |**Bm7**
And then there was time for all the wrong rea - sons, oh.

            |**Em7** |**A7sus4**   **A7**   ‖
But, oh, time   is often on my side, but I give it to you.   Oh, boy.

Chorus 3

Dmaj7
     Sleep all, we sleep all day,
Bm7 |**Em7**
  Sleep all, we sleep all day over.
   |**A7sus4**   **A7**
La - din - din - din - da, okay.
      |**Dmaj7** |
So, why don't we,   sleep all, we sleep all day?
Bm7 |**Em7** |**A7sus4** **A7**
  Sleep all, we sleep all day over   and over.

Verse 5

      ‖**Dmaj7** |
  She said, "What would your mother think of all this?
Bm7 |
  How would your father react? Oh, Lord.
Em7 |**A7sus4**   **A7**
  Would he take it all back, what they've done?"
       |**Dmaj7** |
"No way," they said. "Take it, take it, take it," he said.
Bm7 |**Em7**
"Make it, don't break it with your own two hands."
   |**A7sus4**   **A7**
Said that   was my old man, and he said,
   |**Em7** |**G**   ‖**Dmaj7**
"If all, all is grounded, you should go make a mountain out of it.

Outro

|Bm7 |Em7

Lord, go make a mountain out of it, go   on and on and on   and on.

         |A7sus4   A7 |Dmaj7 |Bm7

Well, you should go   on, make a mountain out of   it.

    |Em7 |A7sus4   A7

Hey, love. Go on, go   on and go on

    |Dmaj7 |

And go on and make a mountain.

Bm7 |Em7

   Go on and make a mountain, go   on.

     |A7sus4   A7 |Dmaj7 | ||

You should go   on and make a mountain out of it.

Too Much Food

Words and Music by
Jason Mraz

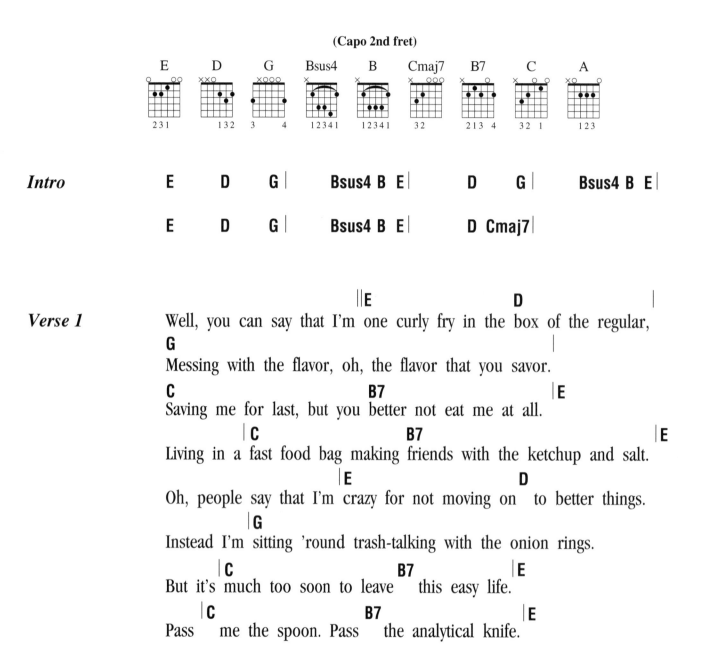

(Capo 2nd fret)

E   D   G   Bsus4   B   Cmaj7   B7   C   A

Intro E   D   G│   **Bsus4 B E**│   D   G│   **Bsus4 B E**│

E   D   G│   **Bsus4 B E**│   D Cmaj7│

Verse 1

‖E   D   │
Well, you can say that I'm one curly fry in the box of the regular,
G   │
Messing with the flavor, oh, the flavor that you savor.
C   B7   │E
Saving me for last, but you better not eat me at all.
│C   B7   │E
Living in a fast food bag making friends with the ketchup and salt.
│E   D
Oh, people say that I'm crazy for not moving on   to better things.
│G
Instead I'm sitting 'round trash-talking with the onion rings.
│C   B7   │E
But it's much too soon to leave   this easy life.
│C   B7   │E
Pass   me the spoon. Pass   the analytical knife.

Chorus 1

                         ‖ **E**
'Cause you're about to get   cut up and get cut down.

  |**G** |**A**
It's all about the wordplay, all about the sound in the tone   of my voice.

                       |**E**
You gotta let me make my choice   alone before my food gets cold.

        |**E**
Better   shut up or get shot down.

   |**G** |
It's all about the know-how, all just a matter of taste.

A |**E**   ‖
   Stop telling me the way I gotta play now.   Too much food on my plate.

Interlude 1   **E**   **D**   **G**| **Bsus4 B E**| **D Cmaj7**|

Verse 2

                           ‖**E**   **D**
Well, believe it or not,   I supersized my sights   on the surprise

           |**G**
In the cereal box. My stomach's smaller than my eyes.

    |**C**   **B7** |**E**
So I went to see the doctor and he said turn my head and then cough.

                 |**C**   **B7** |**E**
I didn't listen to what   he said. Instead,   I couldn't wait to get off.

              |**E**   **D**
He said I can have this but I can't have that.

           |**G**
I should keep wishing I was living the life of a cat

   |**C**   **B7** |**E**
But   I ain't the one whose gon - na be missing the feast,

             |**C**   **B7** |**E**
Just like you   ain't the one who seems   to be calming the beast.

Chorus 2

‖E
Now you're about to get   cut up and get cut down.

|G |A
It's all about the wordplay, all about the sound in the tone   of my voice.

|E
You gotta let me make my choice   alone before my food gets cold.

|E
You better   shut up or get shot down.

|G |
It's all about the know-how, all just a matter of taste.

A |
Stop telling me the way that I gotta play.

E   ‖
You're putting too much food on my plate. Come on.

Interlude 2   E   D   G| Bsus4 B E| D   G|

G Oh, now. **Bsus4 B E**| D   G|

G Said, "Yeah." **Bsus4 B E**| D Cmaj7|

Bridge

‖B7 |
Well, if you are what you eat, in my case   I'll be sweet,

|C |G |B7
So come   and   get   some.

|B7 |C |D
I'm so o - o - ver it.

Chorus 3

‖E

’Cause you’re about to get   cut up and get cut down.

|G |

It’s all about the know-how, all just a matter of taste.

A |

Stop telling me the way that I gotta play.

E   ‖

You put too much food on my plate. Come on.

Outro

E |

Get up to get, get it and get down.

G |

Get up to get, get it and get down.

A |

Get up to get, get it and up. Well, come on.

E |

Get up, get up, get up. Well, come on.

E |

Get up to get, get it and get some.

G |

Get up to get, get it and get some.

A |

Get up to get, get it and get some.

E | D   G |

There’s too much food on my plate. Come on.

G   Bsus4   B E | D   G |
Yeah, yeah, yeah, yeah, yeah.

G   Bsus4   B E | D   G |
Well, come on, come on,   come on,   come on.

G   Bsus4   B E | D Cmaj7 | ‖
Ya - da - da - da.

Absolutely Zero

Words and Music by
Jason Mraz

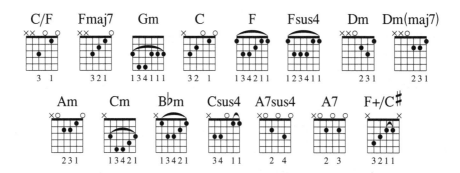

Intro   **C/F** |**Fmaj7** |**C/F** |**Fmaj7** ||

Verse 1

    C/F |**Fmaj7** |
You,   you were a friend.

    C/F |**Fmaj7**
You were a friend of mine. I let you spend   the night.

                  |**Gm** |**C**
You see, how it was my fault.

          |**C/F** |**Fmaj7** |
Of course, it was mine.

    C/F |**Fmaj7**
I'm   too hard at work.

     |**C/F** |**Fmaj7**
Have you ever heard of anything so ab - surd

          |**Gm** |**C**
Ever in your life?

            |**F**   **Fsus4** |**F** ||
I'm sorry for wasting your time.

Chorus 1

   Dm   **|Dm(maj7)**
Who am I to say this situa   -   tion isn't great
                     |Am
When it's my job   to make the most of it?
 |Cm   **|Gm**
Of course, I didn't know that it would hap - pen to me.
  |B♭m   **|C/F**   **|Fmaj7**   **||**
Not   that easy.

Verse 2

   C/F   **|Fmaj7**
Hey,   what's that you say?
              |C/F   **|Fmaj7**
You're not blaming me for anything. Well, that's great,
                     |Gm
But I don't break that eas - y.
  |C   **|C/F**   **|Fmaj7**
Does it fade away?
               |C/F   **|Fmaj7**
So that's why I'm,   I'm apologiz - ing now
  |C/F   **|Fmaj7**
For telling you I thought that we could make   it.
                  |Gm
I just don't get enough
     |C   **|F**   **Fsus4**   **|F**
To believe that we've both changed.

Chorus 2

```
  ‖Dm                              |Dm(maj7)
So who am I to say this situa   -    tion isn't great?
               |Am
It's my time    to make the most of it.
  |Cm                                    |Gm
Of course, I didn't know that it would hap  -  pen to me.
    |B♭m              |F           |Csus4    C
Not     that easy, no,   no, no, no.
  |Dm                              |Dm(maj7)
If all along the fault is up for grabs,          why can't you have it?
               |Am
If it's for sale,    what is your offer?
    |Cm                              |Gm
I will sell it for no less than what I bought    it for.
    |B♭m              |F           |Csus4   C    |F          |A7sus4  A7
Pay     no more than ab - solutely ze - ro.
```

Bridge

```
  ‖Gm                                   |C
Well, neither one of us deserves the blame
         |F        F+/C♯                 |Dm
Because op - portunities     moved us away.
    |Gm                              |C
It's not an easy thing to learn to play
    |F                     F+/C♯              |Dm
A game   that's made for two,      that's you and me.
                              |B♭m
The rules remain a mystery.
                    |A7sus4   A7
See how it's eas - y.
```

Chorus 3

    ‖**Dm** |**Dm(maj7)**

So, who am I to say this situa   -   tion isn't great?

                   |**Am**

Well, it's our time   to make the most of it.

    |**Cm** |**Gm**

How could we ever know that this would hap - pen to me?

    |**B♭m** |**F** |**Csus4**   **C**

Not   that easy, no, no, ho, ho,

     |**Dm** |**Dm(maj7)**

When all along the fault is up for grabs,   and there you have it.

                  |**Am**

Well, it's for sale.   Go make your offer.

    |**Cm** |**Gm**

Will I sell it for no less than what I bought it for?

     |**B♭m** |**F** |**Csus4**   **C** |**F** |

Pay   no more than ab - solutely ze - ro.

     |**F** | ‖

Love, love.

On Love, in Sadness

Words and Music by
Jason Mraz and Jenny Keane

(Capo 2nd fret)

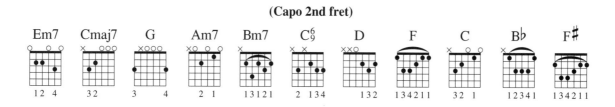

Em7   Cmaj7   G   Am7   Bm7   C⁶₉   D   F   C   B♭   F♯

Intro

| **Em7** | | | | **Cmaj7** | | | | |

| **Em7** | | | | **Cmaj7** | | | | |

Verse 1

‖ **G** | | |
Sing about that, oh, love, it's a brittle madness.
Am7 | |
I sing about it in all my sadness.
Bm7 | **C⁶₉** |
It's not falsified to say that I found God
| **G** | | |
So inevitably well. It still exists,
Am7 | **Bm7**
Pale and fine. I can't dismiss and I won't resist.
| **Bm7** | **C⁶₉** |
And if I die, well, at least I tried.

Copyright © 2002 Goo Eyed Music (ASCAP), Flozkid Music Publishing (ASCAP) and Quiet Span Of Sky Publishing
All Rights for Flozkid Music Publishing Administered by Quiet Span Of Sky Publishing
International Copyright Secured   All Rights Reserved

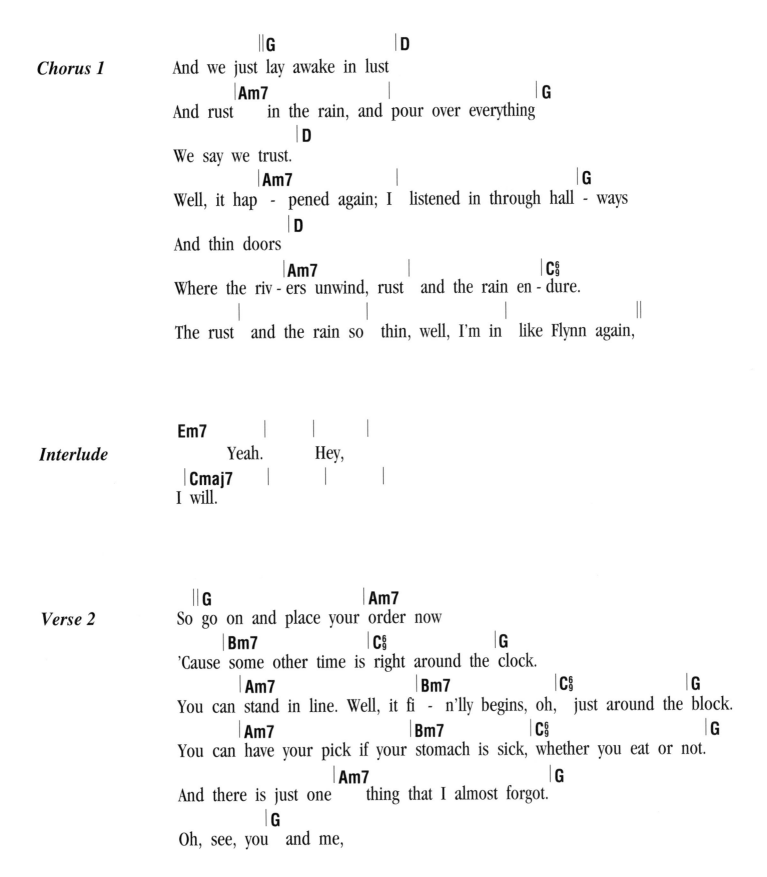

Chorus 1

‖**G** |**D**

And we just lay awake in lust

|**Am7** | |**G**

And rust   in the rain, and pour over everything

                                   |**D**

We say we trust.

                    |**Am7** | |**G**

Well, it hap - pened again; I listened in through hall - ways

                         |**D**

And thin doors

                    |**Am7** | |**C$_9^6$**

Where the riv - ers unwind, rust   and the rain en - dure.

            | | | ‖

The rust   and the rain so   thin, well, I'm in   like Flynn again,

Interlude

Em7 | | |

          Yeah.   Hey,

|**Cmaj7** | | |

I will.

Verse 2

‖**G** |**Am7**

So go on and place your order now

     |**Bm7** |**C$_9^6$** |**G**

'Cause some other time is right around the clock.

          |**Am7** |**Bm7** |**C$_9^6$** |**G**

You can stand in line. Well, it fi - n'lly begins, oh,   just around the block.

          |**Am7** |**Bm7** |**C$_9^6$** |**G**

You can have your pick if your stomach is sick, whether you eat or not.

                         |**Am7** |**G**

And there is just one   thing that I almost forgot.

                    |**G**

Oh, see, you   and me,

Chorus 2

```
         ‖G                D
We just lay awake in lust
      |Am7             |                    |G
And rust    in the rain, and pour over everything
                   |D
We say we trust.
          |Am7            |                   |G
Well, it hap - pened again; I  listened in through hall - ways
                 |D
And thin doors
         |Am7            |                |G
Where the riv - ers unwind, the rivers unwind so eas - y.
    |D                          |G        |
Oh,  these are the comforts that be.
```

Bridge

```
              ‖F           |C          |B♭           |F
You see, well, I'm feeling luck - y. Oh, well,   maybe that's just me.
        |F          |C          |B♭               |F
Well, you'd  be so proud of me. Oh , well,   if you could only  see
        |F                   |C          |B♭                  |
How we're  gonna grow on up to be. Ah, yes, we   are thick as thieves.
N.C. F  F♯   |G   |Am7  |Bm7   |C⁶₉    |G      |Am7     |G        |
   Scat sing...
```

Repeat Verse 1

Chorus 3

```
        ‖G                     |D
```
And we just lay awake in lust
```
          |Am7               |                    |G
```
And rust in the rain, and pour over everything
```
                      |D
```
We say we trust.
```
              |Am7               |              |G
```
Well, it hap - pened again; I listened in through hall - ways
```
                      |D
```
And thin doors
```
              |Am7               |            |C⁶₉
```
Where the riv - ers unwind, rust and the rain en - dure.
```
        |C⁶₉                    |           |
```
The rust and the rain endure. I'm sure because
```
    |G               |D
```
I'm in so far to know
```
                  |Am7               |
```
The measure of love ain't loss. Love will never ever be
```
    |G               |D
```
In so far to know
```
                  |Am7               |
```
The measure of love ain't loss. Love will never ever be
```
    |G               |D
```
In so far to know
```
                  |Am7               |              |C⁶₉      |
```
The measure of love ain't loss. Love will never ever be lost on me.
```
        |C⁶₉                |                    ‖
```
Oh, not tonight. See, love will never ever be lost


```
        Em7        |          |          |                    |Cmaj7          |
```
Outro
    On me. Love will never ever be lost on me.
```
        Cmaj7        |          |
```
Love will not be,
```
        Cmaj7                    |Em7          |
```
Love will never be lost on me.
```
        Em7        |        |Cmaj7      |        |        |        ‖
```
Love will not be lost on me.

No Stopping Us

Words and Music by
Jason Mraz

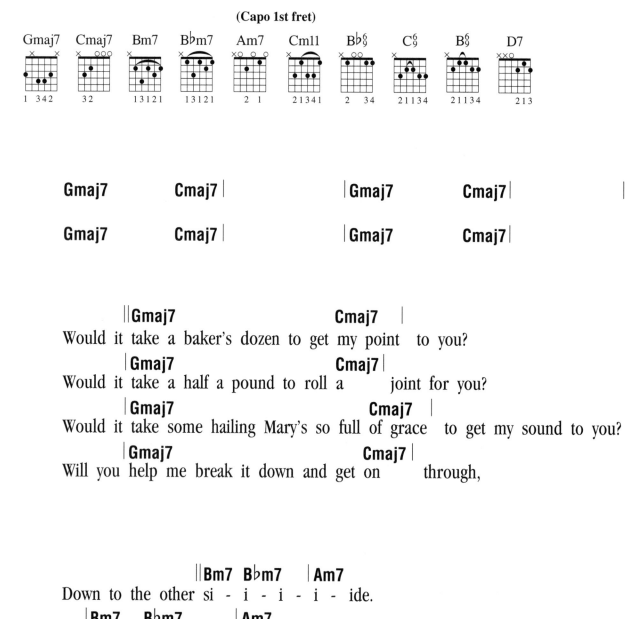

(Capo 1st fret)

Gmaj7   Cmaj7   Bm7   B♭m7   Am7   Cm11   B♭$^6_9$ C$^6_9$ B$^6_9$ D7

Intro   **Gmaj7**   **Cmaj7** | | **Gmaj7**   **Cmaj7**| |

          Gmaj7   **Cmaj7** | | **Gmaj7**   **Cmaj7**|

Verse 1

          ‖**Gmaj7**   **Cmaj7** |
Would it take a baker's dozen to get my point to you?
        |**Gmaj7**   **Cmaj7**|
Would it take a half a pound to roll a   joint for you?
        |**Gmaj7**   **Cmaj7** |
Would it take some hailing Mary's so full of grace to get my sound to you?
        |**Gmaj7**   **Cmaj7** |
Will you help me break it down and get on   through,

Chorus 1

          ‖**Bm7 B♭m7** |**Am7** |
Down to the other si - i - i - i - ide.
      |**Bm7**   **B♭m7** |**Am7** |
It's easy if you only try, try, try, try.
        |**Bm7**   **B♭m7** |**Am7** |
Oh well, don't lie down on the job,   oh, no.
      |**Cm11** | |**Gmaj7**   **Cmaj7** |
Because once we hit the top there's no stopping us   now.
Cmaj7 |**Gmaj7**   **Cmaj7** |
      Ain't no stopping us.

Verse 2

      ‖**Gmaj7**   **Cmaj7** |
Should I address all my letters to the well   to be?

      |**Gmaj7**   **Cmaj7**|
Should I say return to sender's just a   well be done?

      |**Gmaj7**
Should I better not take it so personally

Cmaj7 |
If   all the good loving is never received?

    |**Gmaj7**   **Cmaj7** |
Baby, if it was me, well, I wouldn't think twice.

Chorus 2

     ‖**Bm7 B♭m7** |**Am7**
No, not I, I, I, I, I.

    |**Bm7**   **B♭m7** |**Am7**
It's easy if you only try, try, try.

       |**Bm7**   **B♭m7** |**Am7**
Oh, well, don't lie down on the job   or worse.

    |**Cm11** | |**Gmaj7**   **Cmaj7**|
Because once we hit the top there's no stopping us   now.

Cmaj7 |**Gmaj7**   **Cmaj7**|
    There's no stopping us.

Cmaj7 |**Gmaj7**   **Cmaj7** |
    There's no stopping us   now.

Cmaj7 |**Gmaj7**   **Cmaj7** |
    No stopping us.

Bridge

$\|$ B♭$^6_9$ $\quad\quad\quad\quad$ | $\quad\quad\quad\quad\quad\quad\quad\quad\quad\quad$ | C$^6_9$

Oo, I will   drive a   thousand   miles, or I'll meet you at the station.

| C$^6_9$ $\quad\quad\quad\quad\quad$ B$^6_9$ | B♭$^6_9$ $\quad\quad\quad\quad$ |

If only you would take a va - cation   from this   thing you have created,

| C$^6_9$ $\quad\quad\quad\quad\quad\quad\quad\quad\quad$ | D7 $\quad\quad\quad$ $\|$

I promise   to make   it worth your while.

Interlude

Gmaj7 $\quad\quad$ Cmaj7 | $\quad\quad\quad\quad\quad\quad\quad\quad\quad\quad\quad\quad\quad\quad$ | Gmaj7 $\quad\quad$ Cmaj7 | $\quad\quad\quad\quad$ |

You know, you know that I'll try.

Gmaj7 $\quad\quad$ Cmaj7 | $\quad\quad\quad\quad\quad\quad\quad$ | Gmaj7 $\quad\quad$ Cmaj7 |

Outro

$\|$ Bm7 $\quad$ B♭m7

So, come on, try,   try.

| Am7

Baby, baby, won't you try.

| Bm7 $\quad$ B♭m7 $\quad\quad\quad$ | Am7

It's easy if you do not run.

| Bm7 $\quad\quad$ B♭m7 $\quad\quad\quad$ | Am7

Well, I promise you you'll have your fun, fun.

| Cm11 $\quad\quad\quad\quad\quad\quad$ | $\quad\quad\quad\quad$ | Gmaj7

Because once we hit the top we've just   begun.

| Cmaj7 $\quad\quad\quad\quad\quad\quad$ | Gmaj7 $\quad\quad$ Cmaj7 |

Oo,   there's no stopping us.

Cmaj7 $\quad\quad\quad\quad\quad\quad$ | Gmaj7 $\quad\quad$ Cmaj7 |

There's no stopping us,   yeah.

Cmaj7 $\quad\quad\quad\quad\quad\quad$ | Gmaj7 $\quad\quad$ Cmaj7 | $\quad\quad$ $\|$

There's no stopping us.

The Boy's Gone

Words and Music by
Jason Mraz

(Capo 4th fret)

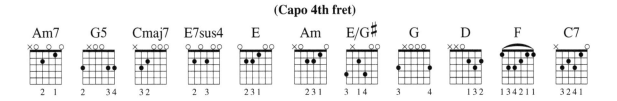

Am7   G5   Cmaj7   E7sus4   E   Am   E/G#   G   D   F   C7

Intro   **Am7** |**G5** |**Cmaj7** |**E7sus4** **E** |

               Am7 |**G5** |**Cmaj7** |**E7sus4**

               E   ‖**Am7** |**G5**
               The boy's   gone.

                            |**Cmaj7** |**E7sus4**
               The boy's gone   home.

               E |**Am7** |**G5**
               The boy's   gone.

                            |**Cmaj7** | ‖
               The boy's gone   home.

Verse 1

```
        Am7                    |G5                              |Cmaj7
            What will hap - pen to a face in the crowd
                                 |E7sus4      E      |
    When it finally gets too crowded?
        Am7                    |G5                              |Cmaj7
            And what will hap - pen to the origins of sounds
                                     |E7sus4          |E
    After all the sounds have sounded?
                        |Am7                          |E/G♯
    Well, I hope      I never have to see that day,
                        |G                        |D
    But, by God, I know it's headed our way.
                        |F              |E7sus4
    So I better be happy now
                  E      |Am7           |G5
    That the boy's go - ing  home.
                        |Cmaj7          |E7sus4      |E      ||
    The boy's gone         home.
```

Verse 2

```
        Am7                        |G5
            And what becomes     of a day
                |Cmaj7                    |E7sus4      E      |
    For those        who rage against         it?
        Am7                        |G5                      |Cmaj7
            And who will sum     up the phrase for all        left
                        |E7sus4        |E
    Standing 'round in         it?
                        |Am7                              |E/G♯
    Well, I suppose     we'll all make our judgment calls.
                        |G                          |D
    We'll walk it alone,  stand up tall, then march  to the fall.
                        |F              |E7sus4
    And we better be    happy now
                  E      |Am7           |G5
    That we'll all go      home.
                        |Cmaj7          |E7sus4  E
    Yeah, we'll all go       home.
```

Bridge 1

```
  ‖Am                        |E/G♯
Be so happy with the way you are.
          |G                      |D
Just be hap - py that you made it this far.
          |F                |
Go on, be   happy now.
          |E7sus4              |E
Please, be happy now.
```

Bridge 2

```
              ‖Am            |C7          |F            |E7sus4
Because you say that this, this is some - thing else,      alright,
E         |Am        |C7              |F              |E7sus4
I say that this, this is   something else.      Well, all right.
E         |Am            |C7                |F              |E7sus4
You say that this, oh,  this   is something, this  is something else.
    E          |Am                  |C7
Oo,  thi - di - di this    is, oh, thi - di - di this    is, yeah,
              |F                    |E7sus4   |E
Di - di - di - di this  is, oh, something else.
```

Bridge 3

```
       ‖Am                          |E/G♯
Well, I tried     to live my life and lived it so well.
              |G                       |D
But when it's all o - ver is it heaven or is it hell?
           |F              |E7sus4
See, I better be happy now
     E      |Am7       |G5
That no one can     tell.
              |Cmaj7   |E7sus4
Say, nobody knows.
```

Outro

```
    E            ‖Am                          |E/G♯
I'm gonna be hap - py with the way that I am.
                              |G                      |D
I'm gonna be hap - py with all that I stand    for.
                      |F            |E7sus4
And I'm gonna be  happy now
          E      |Am7        |G5
'Cause the boy's go - ing home.
              |Cmaj7        |E7sus4
The boy's gone        home.
  E            |Am7        |G5        |Cmaj7
Yeah, the boy's
          |E7sus4
Going home.
  E            |Am7        |G5        |Cmaj7
Yeah, the boy's
          |E7sus4
Going home.
  E            |Am7        |G5        |Cmaj7
Yeah, the boy's
          |E7sus4    E    |Am      ‖
Going home.
```

Tonight, Not Again

Words and Music by
Jason Mraz and Jenny Keane

(Capo 3rd fret)

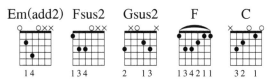

Em(add2) Fsus2 Gsus2   F   C

1 4   1 3 4 2 1 3   1 3 4 2 1 1   3 2 1

Intro   Em(add2) |Fsus2 |Em(add2) |Fsus2 |Em(add2) |Fsus2 |Em(add2) |Fsus2

Verse 1

    || Em(add2) |Fsus2
The night,   she brushed her hand upon my   flushed cheek;

Em(add2) |Fsus2
        Smelled of childhood, remnants of a dust - y weeping willow.

Em(add2) |Fsus2
        Clouds soothe, they're shredded by the calico;

    |Em(add2) |Fsus2
Were oh so vast and quick as I was on   my own now.

Em(add2) |Fsus2 |Em(add2) |Fsus2 ||

Verse 2

Em(add2) |Fsus2
      And this time, like every other time,   I believe that I never find

Em(add2) |Fsus2
      Another sweet little girl with sequined sea   foam eyes,

Em(add2) |Fsus2 |Em(add2)
Ocean-lapping voice, smile coy as the brightest quiet span of   sky.

   |Fsus2
And I'm all alone again   tonight.

   |Em(add2) |Fsus2
Not again, not again, not again.

   |Em(add2) |Fsus2
Not again, not again, not   again. Mm.

Chorus 1

```
          ‖Gsus2      |                              |F
Mm,          oo.            And  don't  it  feel  al - right?
                    |C
And  don't  it  feel  so   nice?
          |Gsus2            |F            |C                    |Em(add2)
Love  -  ly,   love  -  ly,   love  -  ly.  Say,  say  it  again.
          |Fsus2                    |Em(add2)  |Fsus2
Ah,          lovely.  Say  it  again.           Ah.
```

Verse 3

```
          ‖Em(add2)          |Fsus2
Well,  I'm            unable  to  inhale  all  the  riches
          |Em(add2)                          |Fsus2
As  I'm            awkward  as  a  wound  on  my  bones.
                |Em(add2)                      |Fsus2
Still,  I've  got           cobblestone  joints  and  plate  glass  points,
          |Em(add2)                    |Fsus2
As  I'm  all  by  myself  tonight.  Not  a - gain,  not  again.
```

Chorus 2

```
          ‖Gsus2      |                              |F
Oo,          oo.            And  don't  it  feel  al - right?
                    |C
And  don't  it  feel  so   nice?
          |Gsus2            |F            |C
Love  -  ly,   love  -  ly,   love  -  ly.
          |Gsus2            |
Say-ay  -   ay  -  ay - ay.
```

Bridge

                  ‖**F** |**C**

And if you should nervously break down when its time for the shakedown,

         |**Gsus2**

Would you   take it?

            |**F** |**C**

It's when you cry just a little but you laugh in the middle

          |**Gsus2**

That you've   made it.

             |**F** |**C**

And don't it feel al - right? And don't it feel so nice?

      |**Gsus2** | |**F** |**C** |

Love,   love, love, love.   *Scat sing...*

Gsus2 | |**F** |**C**

Interlude

                    ‖**Em(add2)** |**Fsus2** |**Em(add2)**

Say it, say it, say it again.   Love,   love.

    |**Fsus2** |**Em(add2)** |**Fsus2** |**Em(add2)** |**Fsus2**

Love.   Love,   so lovely,   lovely to do it again.

    |**Em(add2)** |**Fsus2** |**Em(add2)** |**Fsus2**

It's so love - ly to do it again.

    |**Em(add2)** |**Fsus2**

Again,   oh, loving again.

    |**Em(add2)** |**Fsus2** |**Gsus2** | |

It's coming again.   It's coming again.

F |**C** |**Gsus2** | |**F** |**C** |**Gsus2** |**F** |**C**

Scat sing...

Outro

                            ‖Em(add2)   **|Fsus2**
Say it, say it, say it again.   Oh,

   |Em(add2)   **|Fsus2**   **|Em(add2)**
So   beautiful.   Tonight,

                    |Fsus2   **|Em(add2)**   **|Fsus2**   **|**
It's coming again.   Love,   lovely.

Em(add2)   **|Fsus2**   **|Em(add2)** **|Fsus2**   **|**
Love, love. *Scat sing...*

Em(add2)   **|Fsus2**   **|Em(add2)**   **|Fsus2**   **‖**
                                    Lovely.

Life Is Wonderful

Words and Music by
Jason Mraz

(Tune down one half step; low to high: E♭-A♭-D♭-G♭-B♭-E♭)

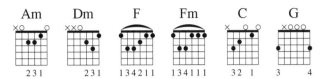

Am   Dm   F   Fm   C   G

Verse 1

‖**Am** |
It takes a crane to build   a crane.
|**Dm** |
It takes two floors to make a   story.
|**F**
It takes an egg to make a hen.
|**Fm**
It takes a hen to make an egg.
|**C** |**G**
There is no end to what I'm   saying.

Verse 2

‖**Am** |
It takes a thought to make   a word.
|**Dm** |
And it takes some words to make an   action.
|**F**
And it takes some work to make it work.
|**Fm**
It takes some good to make it hurt.
|**C** |**G**   ‖
It takes some bad for satis - faction.

Chorus 1

Am |Dm |
Ah, la, la, la, la, la, la. Life   is wonderful.
G |C |
Ah, la, la, la, la, la, la. Life   goes full circle.
Am |Dm |
   Ah, la, la, la, la. Life   is wonderful.
G | |Am | | |
Ah, la, la, la, la.   Mm.

Verse 3

                          ‖Am |
It takes a night to make it   dawn.
                       |Dm |
And it takes a day to make you yawn, brother.
                     |F
And it takes some old to make you young.
                   |F
It takes some cold to know the sun.
               |C |G
It takes the one to have the other.

Verse 4

                        ‖Am |
And it takes no time to fall in love.
            |Dm |
But it takes you years to know what love is.
                   |F
And it takes some fears to make you trust.
                 |F
It takes those tears to make it rust.
             |C |G   ‖
It takes the dust to have it pol - ished.   Yeah.

Chorus 2

Am |Dm |

Ah, la, la, la, la, la. Life   is wonderful.

G |C |

    Ah, la, la, la, la, la. Life   goes full circle.

Am |Dm |

    Ah, la, la, la, la, la. Life   is wonderful.

G | |Am | | |

    Ah, la, la, la.   It is,   it is so …

                  |Am | | |

And it is   so …

Verse 5

                              ‖Am |

It takes some silence to make sound.

                        |Dm |

And it takes a loss before you found it.

                        |F

And it takes a road to go no - where.

                        |Fm

It takes a toll to make you care.

                 |C |G   ‖

It takes a hole to make a mountain.

Chorus 3

Am |Dm |

Ah, la, la, la, la, la. Life   is wonderful.

G |C |

    Ah, la, la, la, la, la. Life   goes full circle.

Am |Dm |

    Ah, la, la, la, la, la. Life   is wonderful.

G |C |

    Ah, la, la, la, la, la. Life   is meaningful.

Am |Dm |

    Ah, la, la, la, la, la, la, la. Life is wonderful.

G |

    Ah, la, la, la, la, la.

Outro

‖**Am** | | |
It is   so   wonder - ful.

|**Am** |
And it is   so meaning - ful.

|**Am** |
It is   so wonder - ful.

|**Am** | | ‖
It is   meaning - ful.

Wordplay

Words and Music by
Jason Mraz and Kevin Kadish

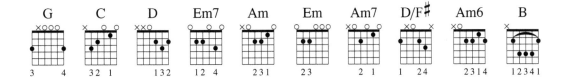

Intro G C |D |G C |D

Verse 1

           ||**Em7**   **G**
I've been all   around the world. I've been a new sensation.
         |**Am**
But it doesn't really matter in this g-generation.
       |**Em7**   **G**
The sophomore slump is an uphill battle,
       |**Am**
And someone said that ain't my scene.
             |**Em7**   **G** |
'Cause they need a new song like a new religion, music for the television.
Am
I can't do the long division. Someone do the math
     |**Em7**   **G** |
'Fore the record label puts me on the shelf up in the freezer.
Am
Got to find another way to live the life of leisure.
       |**Em**   **G**
So I drop my top, mix and I mingle.
     |**Am7** ||
Is everybody ready for the single? And it goes:

Chorus 1

```
G       C           |D
```
La, la, la, la, la.

                            |

Now, listen closely to the verse I lay.
```
G       C       |D
```
  La, la, la, la, la.

                   |

It's all about the wordplay.
```
G       C       |D
```
  I, la, la, la, love

The wonderful thing it does because,
```
  |Em7                                      D/F♯
```
Be - cause I am the wizard of oohs and ahs and fa la la's,
```
      |C                                          |G     C     |D
```
Yeah, the Mister A to Z. They say I'm all about the wordplay.

Verse 2
```
                                      || Em7
```
When it's time to get ill,
```
                              G
```
I got your remedy for those who don't remember me.
```
      |Am
```
Well, let me introduce you to my style.
```
|Em7                           G
```
I try to keep a jumble and the lyrics never mumble
```
          |Am
```
When the music's making people tongue-tied.
```
          |Em7                         G                    |
```
You want a new song like a new religion, music for the television.
```
Am
```
I can't do the long division. Someone do the math
```
          |Em7                         G                |
```
'Fore the people write me off like I'm a one-hit wonder.
```
Am
```
Gotta find another way to keep from going under.
```
          |Em          Tacet
```
Pull out the stops. Got your attention.
```
  |Am7                                              ||
```
I guess it's time again for me to mention the wordplay.

Chorus 1

G   C |D

La, la, la, la, la.
                                        |

Now, listen closely to the verse I lay.

G   C |D

  La, la, la, la, la.
                            |

It's all about the wordplay.

G   C |D

  I, la, la, la, love

The wonderful thing it does because,

  |Em7   D/F♯

Be - cause I am the wizard of oohs and ahs and fa la la's,

         |C |

Yeah, the Mister A to Z. They say I'm all about the wordplay.

Bridge

          ||Am6

I built a bridge across a stream of consciousness.

                     |B

It always seems to be flowing,

But I don't know which way my brain is going.

      |Em   D

All the ryhming and the timing keeps the melodies inside me,

   |C

Ever climbing till I'm running out of air.

        |Am6 |

Are you pre - pared to take a dive into the deep end of my head?

B | ||

  Are you listening to a single word I've said?

Chorus 2

```
      G       C        |D
La, la, la, la, la.
                                 |
Now, listen closely to the words I say.
      G       C        |D
  La, la, la, la, la.
                             |
I'm sticking to the wordplay.
      G       C          |D
  I, la, la, la, love

The wonderful thing it does because,
  |Em7                                D/F♯
Be - cause I am the wizard of oohs and ahs and fa la la's,
          |C                                    ‖
Yeah, the Mister A to Z. They say I'm all about the wordplay.
```

Chorus 3

```
      G       C        |D
La, la, la, la, la.
                         |
I'm all about the wordplay
      G       C        |D
  La, la, la, la, la.
                         |
Sticking with the wordplay.
      G       C          |D
  I, la, la, la, love,

I love the wonderful thing it does because,
  |Em7                          D/F♯
Be - cause the oohs and ahs and fa la la's. Fall back in love
          |C                              |        ‖
With the Mister A to Z. They say it's all about the wordplay.
```

Geek in the Pink

Words and Music by
Jason Mraz, Kevin Kadish, Scott Storch and Ian Sheridan

(Capo 1st fret)

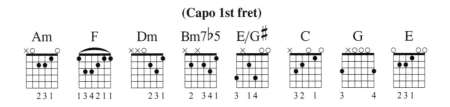

Am   F   Dm   Bm7♭5   E/G♯   C   G   E

Intro

| **Am** | **F** | |
Do, do, do, do, do, do,   do, do, do, do, do.
| **Dm** | **Bm7♭5** | **E/G♯** | ‖
Do, do, do, do, do, do,   do, do, do, do, do.

Verse 1

   Am |
   Well, let the geek in the pink take a stab at it.
F |
   If you like the way I'm thinking, baby, wink at it.
Dm |
   I may be skinny at times, but I'm fat full of rhymes.
C   **G**
   Pass me the mic and I'm-'ll grab at it.
   |**Am**
Well, isn't it delicious crazy way that I'm kissing this.
   |**F** |
Baby, listen to this. Don't wanna miss it while it's hittin'.
Dm
   Sometimes you gotta fit in to get in,
   |**C**   **E/G♯** ‖
But   don't ever quit 'cause soon I'm gonna let you in. Well, see,

Chorus 1

Am |F
I don't care what you might think about me.
        |Dm |Bm7♭5   E/G♯
You'll get   by without me if you want.
               |Am
Well, I could be the one to take you home.
           |F
Baby, we could rock the night alone.
         |Dm
If we never get down, it wouldn't be a let-down.
          |Bm7♭5   E
But, sugar, don't for-get what you already know:
          |Am
That I could be the one to turn you out.
        |F
We could be the talk across the town.
          |Dm
Don't judge it by the color, confuse it for another.
       |C   G
You might re-gret what you let slip a-way,
         |Am |F |
Like the geek in the pink. Do, do, do, do, do, do, do, do, do, do, do.
Dm |Bm7♭5   E/G♯
Do, do, do, do, do, do, do,   do, do, do, do, do.

Verse 2

       ‖**Am**

All my re - lationship fodder don't mean to bother nobody.

      |**F** |

But Cupid's automatic must've fired multiple shots at her,

Dm

  Because she fall in love too often; that's what's the matter.

 |**C**   **G**

At least when I'm talking about her, keep a patter to flattery.

   |**Am**

And   she was staring through the doorframe

   |**F** |

And eyeing me down like already a bad boyfriend.

Dm

   Well, she can get her toys out of the drawer, then.

  |**C**   **E/G♯**   ‖

'Cause I ain't comin' home. I don't need that attention. See,

Chorus 2

Am |**F**

I don't care what you might think about me.

  |**Dm** |**Bm7♭5**   **E/G♯**

She'll get   by without me if she wants.

          |**Am**

Well, I could be the one to take her home.

        |**F**

Baby, we could rock the night alone.

        |**Dm**

If we never get down. It wouldn't be a let down.

       |**Bm7♭5**   **E**

But, sugar, don't for - get what you already know:

       |**Am**

That I could be the one to turn you out.

     |**F**

We could be the talk across the town.

        |**Dm**

Don't judge it by the color, confuse it for another.

     |**C**   **G**   ‖

You might re - gret what you let slip a - way.

Bridge

        F |Am
        Hey, baby, look at me go
           |E
From zero to hero.

                     |Am
You better take it from a geek like me.
         |F |Am
Well, I can save you from unoriginal dumb - dumbs

                   |Bm7♭5 |E
Who wouldn't care if you com - plete them or not.

              ||Am
Verse 3
So what? I got a short attention span, a Coke in my hand,
            |F
Because I'd rather have the afternoon relaxing.
          |Dm |
Understand my hip-hop in flip-flops, well, it don't stop with the light rock.
C   G   E/G♯ |
  My shot to mock you kinda puts me in the tight spot.
Am
  The hype is nothing more than hoo-hah,
          |F |
So I'm de - veloping a language and I'm calling it my own.
Dm |
  So, take a peek into the speaker and you'll see what I mean:
C   G   E/G♯ ||
  That on the other side the grass is green - er.

Chorus 3

Am |F

I don't care what you might think about me.

      |Dm |Bm7♭5   E/G♯

You'll get   by without me if you want.

                |Am

Well, I could be the one to take you home.

              |F

Baby, we could rock the night alone.

            |Dm

If we never get down. It wouldn't be a let down.

             |Bm7♭5   E

But, sugar, don't for - get what you already know:

             |Am

That I could be the one to turn you out.

            |F

We could be the talk across the town.

              |Dm

Don't judge it by the color, confuse it for another.

         |C   G

You might re - gret what you let slip a - way,

            |Am |

Like the geek in the pink. Do, do, do, do, do, do,

F |

   Do, do, do, do, do. Well, I'm the geek in the pink.

Dm |Bm7♭5   E/G♯

Do, do, do, do, do, do, do. Geek is the color for fall.

              |Am |

I'm the geek in the pink. Do, do, do, do, do, do,

F |

   Do, do, do, do, do. In the pink, yo.

Dm |C   G

Do, do, do, do, do, do, do. Geek is the color for fall.

              |Am ||

I'm the geek in the pink.

Did You Get My Message?

Words and Music by
Jason Mraz and Dan Wilson

(Tune down one half step; low to high: E♭-A♭-D♭-G♭-B♭-E♭)

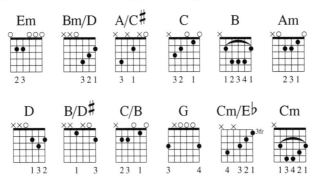

Intro

Em   Bm/D |A/C♯ C B |Em   Bm/D |A/C♯ C B |

Em   Bm/D |A/C♯ C B |Em   Bm/D |A/C♯ C B

Verse 1

‖Em   Bm/D
Did you get my message, the one I left?
     |A/C♯   C
Well, I was trying to condense everything that I meant
B |Em   Bm/D
In a minute or less when I called   to confess
     |A/C♯   C
And make all   of my stresses go bye - bye.
B |Em   Bm/D
Did you get my message? You didn't, I guess,
     |A/C♯   C
'Cause if you did, you would've called me with your sweet intent.
B |Em   Bm/D
And we could give it a rest instead of beating our breast
     |A/C♯   C   B ‖
And making all of the pressure go sky high.

Pre-Chorus 1

```
                                                    |D                    B/D♯
Am      Do  you  ever  wonder  what  happens  to  the  words  that  we  send?
            |Em                          D
Do they bend,    do they break from the flight   that they take
   |A/C♯                                          |Am
And  come  back  together  again  with  a  whole  new  mean - ing
                                    |D              B/D♯
And  a  brand-new  sense,  com - pletely  unrelated  to  the  one  I  sent?
```

Chorus

```
            ‖C                C/B     |Am        D
Did  you  get  my  message?     Ooh,  ooh,  ooh.
            |Em              D      |A/C♯
Oh,  did  you  get  my  message?
            |C                C/B     |Am      D          ‖
Oh,  did  you  get  my  message?  Yeah,  ooh,  ooh,  ooh,    hoo.
```

Verse 2

```
Em        Bm/D
    Uh oh!  Where  did  it  go?
    |A/C♯                                  C              B        |
Must've  bypassed  your  phone  and  flown  right  out  of  the  win - dow.
Em        Bm/D
    Oh  well,  how  can  I  tell?
      |A/C♯                          C              B
Should  I  call  the  operator?  Oh,  maybe  she  knows  the  in - fo
   |Em                  Bm/D
Or  whether  or  not  if  my  message  you  got
      |A/C♯                      C
Was  too  much  or  a  lot  to  re - ply.
            B     |Em                          Bm/D
Why   not  try  this  for  a  fact  (well,  should  you  ever  call  back)?
      |A/C♯                          C            B    ‖
I'd  re - lax  and  be  relieved  of  all  my  panic  attacks.
```

Pre-Chorus 2

```
        G          |C       Cm/E♭        |
Ah, ah, ah, ah, ooh, ooh, ooh, ooh.
        G          |C       Cm/E♭
Ah, ah, ah, ah, ooh, ooh.
```

Repeat Chorus

Interlude

```
        Em      Bm/D          |A/C♯       C
             So, d-d-d-d-do      you now?
             B   |Em      Bm/D              |A/C♯       C
Arr, d-do do do     d-do.      Arr, d-do do ooh.
```

Verse 3

```
        B       ‖Em           Bm/D
Oh, did you get my message, the one I left?
              |A/C♯                    C
Well, I was trying to condense everything   that I meant.
        B     |Em                       Bm/D
Now the moment has passed. (Not much sand in the glass.)
         |A/C♯                  C    B ‖
And I'm standing to lose my mind.
```

Pre-Chorus 3

```
        Am                              |D           B/D♯
      Do you ever wonder what happens to the words that we send?
               |Em                 D
Do they bend,    do they break from the flight   that they take
        |A/C♯                           |Am
And come back together again with a whole new mean - ing

To the matter of our love's defense?
        |D              B/D♯
At least be sympathetic to the time I spent.
```

Repeat Chorus

Outro

‖**G** |**C**   **Cm/E♭**
Did you get my message?

|**G** |**C**   **Cm/E♭**
Did you get my message?

|**G** |
Did you get my message, love,

C   **Cm/E♭**
 That I want to get back with you?

|**G**
Did you get my message, love,

|**C**   **Cm/E♭**
That I want to reconnect with you?

|**G**
Did you get my message now?

|**C**   **Cm**   ‖
So, why don't you answer the phone?

Mr. Curiosity

Words and Music by
Jason Mraz, Lester Mendez and Dennis Morris

(Capo 3rd fret)

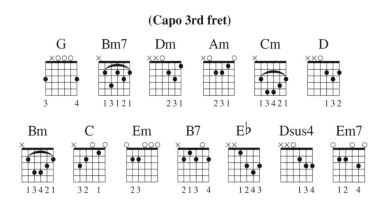

Intro   G |Bm7 |Dm |Am |Cm |G |Am |D   ‖

Verse 1

G |Bm
Hey, Mister Curiosity,

                                        |Dm
Is it true what they've been saying about you?

           |Am
Are you killing me?

              |Cm
You took care of the cat already.

          |G |Am
And for those who think it's heavy, is it the truth

                |D   ‖
Or is it only gos - sip?

Verse 2

```
G                              |Bm
Call it mystery or anything,
                              |Dm
Just as long as you'd call me.
                              |Am
I sent the message on.    Did you get it when I left it?
        |Cm
See, this catastrophic event,
        |G
It wasn't meant to mean no harm.
    |Am                          |D              ||
But to think there's nothing wrong is a prob - lem.
```

Chorus 1

```
C                          |G
  I'm looking for love   this time,
        |Bm                    |Em       D         |
Sounding hopeful but it's making me cry.
C                |G
  Love is a mys - tery.
    |B7            |                        ||
Mister Curious,            come back to me.
```

Verse 3

```
G                              |Bm
  Mister Waiting, ever pa - tient, can't you see
                |Dm
That I'm the same the way you left me?
    |Am
In a hurry to spell-check me.
        |Cm                          |G
And I'm underlined already in envy green and pencil red.
            |Am
And I've for - gotten what you said.
                |D
Will you stop working for the dead
```

Verse 4

```
         ‖G                              |Bm
And re -turn, Mister Curious? Well I need    some inspiration.
         |Dm                           |Am
It's my birthday and I cannot find no cause    for celebration.
         |Cm                    |G
The sce - nario is grave, but I'll be braver when you save me
         |Am                 |D           ‖
From this situation laden with hear - say.
```

Chorus 2

```
C                    |G
   I'm looking for love   this time,
     |Bm                        |Em        D        |
Sounding hopeful but it's making me cry.
C                |G
   And love is a mys - tery.
     |B7                          |              ‖
Mister Curiousity, be Mister Please   Do Come And Find Me.
```

Bridge

```
Em      |Eb    |Em      |Eb        |
                Find,      find me,
Cm      |G      |Cm           |D          |Dsus4    ‖
Find      me,       find   me.
```

Interlude

```
G      |Bm      |Dm      |Am      |Cm      |G      |Am      |D      ‖
```
Operatic falsetto vocal ad lib...

Chorus 3

```
         C                        |G
       I'm  looking  for  love   this  time,
           |Bm                          |Em
Sounding  hopeful  but  it's  making  me  cry,
           D          |C                    |G
Trying  not  to  ask  why.  This  love  is  a mys - tery.
           |B7                         |
Mister  Curiousity,  be  Mister  Please   Do  Come  And  Find  Me.
               |C                        |G
Love  is  blinding  when  the  timing's  never  right.
                     |B7
Or  who  am  I     to  beg  for  difference?
           |Em               D                      |C
Finding  love  in  just  an  in - stant,  well,  I  don't  mind.
                   |G                   |B7
At  least  I've  tried.  Well,  I  tried,
               |B7         |Em7        |              ||
I  tried.
```

Clockwatching

Words and Music by
Jason Mraz, Dennis Morris and Ainslie Henderson

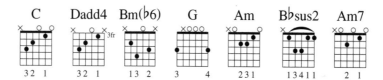

Intro   C |Dadd4 |Bm(♭6) |C | |Dadd4 |Bm(♭6) |C ||

        C |Dadd4 |Bm(♭6) |C |

Verse 1 Take off both your shoes and clothes; I'll follow.

        C |Dadd4 |Bm(♭6) |C |

        Undo corkscrew. Drink from a half of a bro - ken bottle.

        C |Dadd4 |Bm(♭6) |C | ||

         Lately, we're running out of time,   aren't we?

        C |Dadd4 |Bm(♭6) |C |

Verse 2 Smoking often and calling out our guilt - y pleasures.

        C |Dadd4 |Bm(♭6) |C |

        Let's keep talking, anything to stop clockwatching.

        C |Dadd4 |Bm(♭6) |C |

         Lately, we're running out of time. Aren't we?

        C |Dadd4 |Bm(♭6) |C |

         Crazy for running all the time?   M-m-m-m-maybe.

        C |Dadd4 |G | ||

        Let's forget we're running out of time.

Chorus 1

G   Dadd4 | |Am | |

I'm off like an aer - oplane.

G   Dadd4| |Am | |

I'm licking your post - age stamp again.

G   Dadd4| |Am | |

I'm using my right   brain and I'm praying that we don't crash.

B♭sus2   Am7 | |G | |

Who knew I'd come   so fast?

B♭sus2   Am7 | |G | |

But so what if a two - pump chump can't last.

B♭sus2   C |

But I made it to three,

           |G |

And I fore - closed a five-minute   fantasy

           |B♭sus2 |Am7 | |

On a short - lived flight making love   on economy.

Verse 3

||C |Dadd4 |Bm(♭6) |C |

No jumping con - clusions. I don't think there's no   solution.

C |Dadd4 |Bm(♭6) |C |

Let's get backwards and for - get our restless des - tination.

C |Dadd4 |Bm(♭6) |C |

Let's live in the moment just this time.   Could we

C |Dadd4 |Bm(♭6) |C |

Just take one moment of our time?   M-m-m-m-maybe.

C |Dadd4 |G | ||

Let's forget we're running out of time.

Chorus 2

G   Dadd4 | |Am | |
I'm off like an aer - oplane.

G   Dadd4| |Am | |
I'm catching my sec - ond wind again.

G   Dadd4| |Am | |
I'm using my left   brain and I'm righting all my wrongs.

B♭sus2   Am7| |G | |
I'm yearning to turn   you on.

B♭sus2   Am7| |G | |
I've been working on get - ting you off, so get on - board.

B♭sus2   C |
Well, how can I guess   by the subject

|G |
Of the best predicate that's left unsaid?

|B♭sus2 |
When the matter is too delicate,

|Am7 | | | ||
My lone - liness is evident.

Interlude 1   C |Dadd4 |Bm(♭6) |C | |Dadd4 |Bm(♭6) |C

                    ||C
Bridge   And its you;

                |Dadd4 |
You're running through my mind,

Bm(♭6) |C ||
And it makes me crazy, cra-cra-crazy.

72

Interlude 2   **C** |**Dadd4** |**Bm(♭6)** |**C** | |**Dadd4** |**Bm(♭6)** |**C** |

          C |**Dadd4** |**Bm(♭6)** |**C** | |**Dadd4** |**Bm(♭6)** |**C**   ‖

          C |**Dadd4** |**Bm(♭6)** |**C** |
Verse 4 Lady dreamer, you might be the sound - est sleeper.
          C |**Dadd4** |**Bm(♭6)** |**C** | ‖
          Tonight, sleep tight and build your nest upon   my shoulder.

Bella Luna

Words and Music by
Jason Mraz and William Galewood

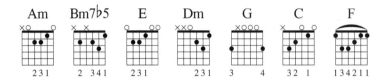

Intro   Am | |Bm7♭5 | | | E |Am | ‖

Verse 1

Am |
Mystery the moon,
 |Bm7♭5 |
A hole in the sky,
 |Bm7♭5 |
A supernatural nightlight,
 |Am |
So full but often wry.
 |Dm |
A pair of eyes,   a closing one,
 |Am |
A chosen child of golden sun.
 |Bm7♭5 |
A marble dog   that chases cars to farthest reaches of the beach
 |E | ‖
And far beyond into the swimming sea of stars.

Interlude 1   Am |Bm7♭5 | E | |Am |Bm7♭5 | E |

Verse 2

‖**Am** |
The cosmic   fish, they love to kiss.
|**Bm7♭5** |
They're giving birth to constellations.
|**Bm7♭5** |
No riffs, and, oh, no reser - vation.
|**Am** | |
If they should fall, you get a wish or dedi - cation.
Dm | |
   May I sug - gest you get the best
Am | |
   For nothing less than you and I.
Bm7♭5 |
      Let's take a chance   as this romance is rising,
|**E** | ‖
Oh, before we lose the lighting.

Chorus 1

Dm |**G** |**C**
         Oh, Bella, Bella, please,
|**F** |**Dm** |
Bella, you   beautiful luna.
Dm |**E** | ‖
   Oh, Bella, do what you   do.

Repeat Interlude 1

Verse 3

‖**Am** |
You are an il‑luminating anchor
|**Bm7♭5** |
Of leagues too infinite in number,
|**Bm7♭5** |
Crashing waves and breaking thunder,
|**Am** | |
Tiding the ebb and flows of hunger.
Dm |
You're dancing naked there for me.
|**Am** |
You ex‑pose all memory. You make the most of boundary.
|**Bm7♭5** |
You're the ghost of royalty imposing love.
|**E**
You are the queen and king com‑bining everything,
|**E**
Inter‑twining like a ring

Pre-Chorus 1

‖**Am** |**Dm**
Around the finger of a girl.
|**G** |**C**
I'm just a singer; you're the world.
|**F**
All I can bring ya
|**Dm** |**E** | ‖
Is the lan‑guage of a lov‑er.

Chorus 2

Am |**Dm** |**G**
Bella Lu‑na,
|**C** |**F**
My beautiful, beautiful moon,
|**Dm** |**E** | ‖
How you swoon me like no oth‑er, oh.

Interlude 2   **Am** | |**Bm7♭5** | | | |**Am** | | |

                      Am | |**Bm7♭5** | | | |**Am** | | ‖

Pre-Chorus 2

Dm | |**Am**

   May I sug - gest you get the best of your wish.

                        |**Am** |**Bm7♭5**

May I insist, at no con - test for little you or smaller I,

      |**Bm7♭5** |**E**

A larger chance at what all there may lie   on the rise,

      |**E**   ‖

On the brink of our lives.

Chorus 3

Dm |**G** |**C**

      Bella, plea - ee - ee - ease,

       |**F** |**Dm** |

Bella, you   beautiful luna,

Dm |**E** | ‖

   Oh, Bella, do what you   do.

Repeat Chorus 2

Outro   **Am** |**Bm7♭5** | **E**| |**Am** |**Bm7♭5** | |**E** |**Am** ‖

Plane

Words and Music by
Jason Mraz and Dennis Morris

(Tune down one half step; low to high: E♭-A♭-D♭-G♭-B♭-E♭)

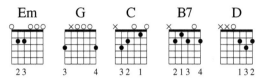

Em   G   C   B7   D

Intro   **Em G |C   B7 |Em   G |C   B7 ||**

Verse 1

Em   **G**
Drain the veins in my head.
　　　　　　　|C　　　　　　　　　　**B7**　　　　　　|
Clean out the reds in my eyes to get   by security lines.
Em   **G**
　　Dear X-ray ma - chine,
　　　　　　　　　|C　　　　　　　　**B7**　　　　　　　|
Pretend you don't know me so well. I won't tell if you lie.
Em   **G**
Cry 'cause the drought's been brought up.
　　　　　　　　|C　　　　　　　　　**B7**
Drinkin' 'cause you're looking so good in your Star - bucks cup.
　　　　|Em　　　　　　　　**G**
I com - plain for the company that I   keep.
　　　　　|C　　　　　　　　　　　　**B7**
The window's for sleeping; rearrange. Well, I'm no - body.

‖C
Well, who's laughing now?
　　　　G
I'm leaving your town again.
B7　　　　　　　　　　　　　　　　　　|C
　　And I'm over the ground that you've been spin - ning.
　　　　　　　G　　　　　　|B7
And I'm up in the air,　so, baby, hell, yeah!
　　　　　　　　　　　　　　|
Well, honey, I can see your house from here.
C　　　　　　G　　　　|
　　If the plane goes　down,　damn,
B7　　　　　　　　　　　　　　　|
　　Well, I'll remember where the love was found.
C　　　　　　　　G　　|B7　　　　‖
　　If the plane goes　down,　damn.

Verse 2

Em　　　　　　　　G
Damn! I should be so lucky.
　　　　　　　　|C
Even only twen - ty-four hours under your touch,
B7
You know I need you so much.
　|Em　　　　　　　　G　　　　　　　　　|C
I,　I cannot wait to call you and tell you that I land - ed
　　　　　　　　　　　　　B7　　　　|
Somewhere and hand you a square　of the airport
Em　　　　　　　　　　G　　　　　　　　　|
　　And walk you through the maze　of the map that I'm gazing at,
C　　　　　　　　B7
Gracefully unnamed and feeling guilty
　　　　　　　　　　|
For the luck and the look that you gave me.
Em　　　　　　　　G
　　You make me somebod - y.
　　　　　|C　　　　　　　B7　　　　‖
Oh, nobody knows　me. Not even me can see it, yet I bet I'm

Chorus 2

```
C                 G           |
    Leaving your town again.
B7                                        |C
    And I'm over the ground that you've been spin - ning.
                        G           |B7
And I'm up in the air,   so, baby, hell, yeah!

                                          |
Well, honey, I can see your house from here.
C                 G           |
    If the plane goes  down,   damn,
B7                                  |
    I'll remember where the love was found.
C                 G           |B7          ||
    If the plane goes  down,   damn.
```

Interlude

```
Em   D   |C         |Em   G   |C   B7
```

Bridge

```
              ||Em    D        |C
You get me high  -  minded.
                 |Em   G   |C   B7    ||
You keep me high.
```

Verse 3

```
       Em          G                   |C
       Flax seeds,   well, they tear me o - pen
                               B7                    |
And supposedly you could crawl right through me.
       Em          G                  |
    Taste  these  teeth,  please,
    C                            B7
    And undress me from the sweaters.
                          |Em              G           |
Better hurry, 'cause I'm   heating upward bound now.
    C                            B7
    Oh, maybe I'll build my house on your cloud.
          |Em        G           |
Here I'm   tumbling    for you,
    C                                  B7                        ||
Stumbling through the work that I have to do. Don't mean to harm you
```

Chorus 3

```
    C                   G          |
    By leaving your town again.
B7                                        |C
    But I'm over the quilt that you've been spin - ning.
                     G            |B7
And I'm up in the air,  so, baby, hell, yeah!
                                     |C
Well, honey, I can see your house from here.
                  G            |
If the plane goes down,    damn,
B7                                    |
    I'll remember where the love was found.
    C            G               |
    If the plane goes  down,    damn,
B7                                    |
    I'll remember where the love was found.
    C         G                  |
    If the plane  goes down,    damn,
B7                                    |
    I'll remember where the love was found.
    C         G            |B7                    ||
    If the plane  goes down, damn,  damn,   damn.
```

Outro   Em G |C   B7

                    |Em   G |C   B7
Damn.
                        |Em   G |C   B7
You get me high.
                            |Em   G |C   B7
You keep me high - minded.
                        |Em   G |C   B7
You get me high.
                            |Em   G |C   B7 |Em ||
You get me high - minded.

O, Lover

Words and Music by
Jason Mraz and Dennis Morris

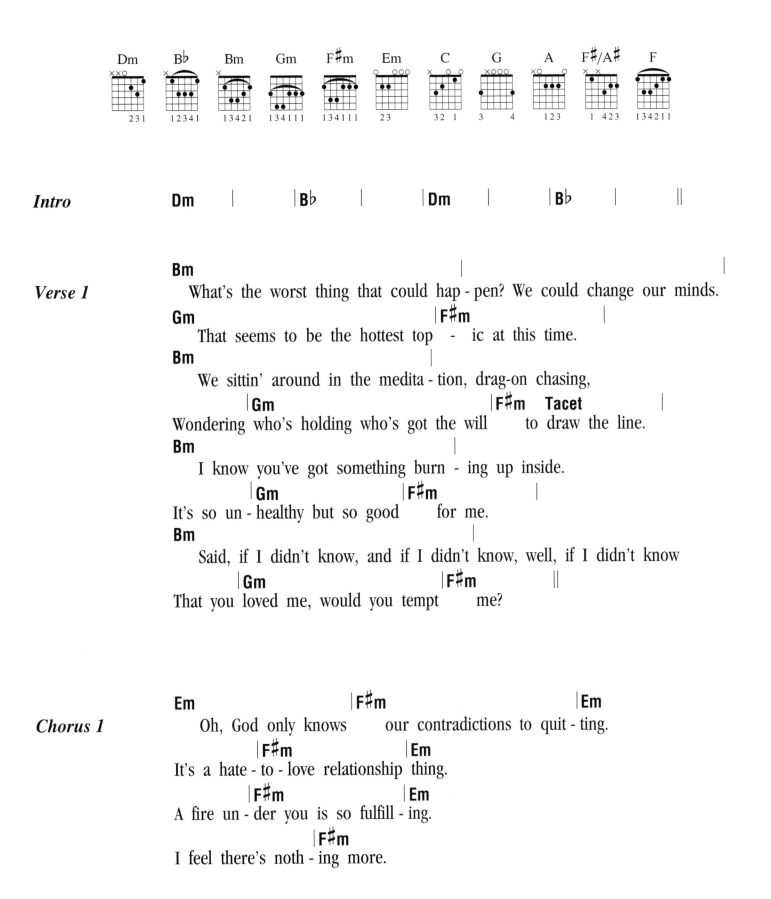

Intro

|: Dm | | Bb | | Dm | | Bb | | :||

Verse 1

Bm
    What's the worst thing that could hap - pen? We could change our minds.
Gm |F#m
    That seems to be the hottest top - ic at this time.
Bm
    We sittin' around in the medita - tion, drag-on chasing,
     |Gm |F#m **Tacet**
Wondering who's holding who's got the will   to draw the line.
Bm
    I know you've got something burn - ing up inside.
    |Gm |F#m
It's so un - healthy but so good   for me.
Bm
    Said, if I didn't know, and if I didn't know, well, if I didn't know
   |Gm |F#m
That you loved me, would you tempt   me?

Chorus 1

Em |F#m |Em
    Oh, God only knows   our contradictions to quit - ting.
    |F#m |Em
It's a hate - to - love relationship thing.
    |F#m |Em
A fire un - der you is so fulfill - ing.
    |F#m
I feel there's noth - ing more.

Verse 2

    ‖**Bm** |

I'm giving, giving you the choke hold.

  |**Gm** |**F♯m**

My flirting with disaster is mod - ern love.

    |**Bm** |

Ooh, you,   you're so bold.

   |**Gm** |**F♯m**

My wanting to kiss you still is not enough.

      |**Bm** |

I'm getting over   all the comments.

       |**Gm** |**F♯m**

Unfriendly statements made by people of non - sense.

     |**Bm** |

I'm getting stronger   by the minute.

     |**Gm** |**F♯m**

And once I slip into position, I'll swing   you

Chorus 2

      ‖**Em**

And turn you all a - round.

     |**F♯m** |**Em**

You are the sweet - est thing I've found since whenev - er.

    |**F♯m** |**Em**

You're the only way my time is measured.

    |**F♯m** |**Em**

You might be the silent type, but you're ad - vertising louder now.

 |**F♯m**   ‖

It's crazy how you're killing me.

Interlude 1

   Dm | **|B♭** |

You're killing me.

Verse 3

```
                      ‖Bm                              |
```
But I like your   red top and matching bottoms.
```
Bm                                              |
```
You know the ones, the ones you've got on.
```
Gm                                    |F♯m                      |
```
Pull 'em over your skinny self, but don't cover your tattoo. *Whoo!*
```
Bm                              |                      |
```
'Cause I like to look at you, yeah.   I love that smell on you.
```
Gm                              |F♯m                      |
```
And I got your special place against   this face for tasting, too.
```
Bm                      |              |
```
And I like it natural;   no need for chemicals.
```
Gm                                    |F♯m                      |
```
Sparking it up my senses, you're making the sense.   You call it sexual.
```
Bm                              |              |
```
And you're going to get yours, my lady.   Might even be today.
```
Gm                              |F♯m                      ‖
```
And it ain't no thing, 'cause I'll be rolling right along with you.

Chorus 3

```
      Em                  |F♯m                              |Em
```
You are the sweet - est thing I've found since whenev - er.
```
            |F♯m                      |Em
```
You're the only way my time is measured.
```
            |F♯m                      |Em
```
You might be the silent type, but you're ad - vertising louder now.
```
      |F♯m                      ‖
```
It's crazy how you're killing me.

Bridge

```
        Bm                              |C
           And give us both a break.
                                    |G                          |A
        And give us back a taste    when the way things were
                    F#/A#            |
        Before they made the laws.
        Bm                              |C
           And give us both a chance.
                                    |G
        But it won't be the last    romance,
                    |A                      F#/A#              ||
        'Cause when the weekend starts, the guilty party's on.
```

Interlude 2

```
        Dm            |        |B♭        |        |Dm        |        |

        B♭            |        |F        |        |A        |F#/A#        ||
```

Outro

```
        Bm                              |                          Gm|
           Weekend party's over.    Don't stop; let's get clos - er.
        Gm                          F#m|                          Bm |
           Friday, got cold should - er.    Monday, got a new compo - sure.
        Bm                              |                          Gm|
           Weekend party's over.    Don't stop; let's get low - er.
        Gm                          F#m|                  Bm |
           I won't blow your cov - er.    Opportunistic lov - er.
        Bm                              |                          Gm|
           Weekend party's over.    Don't stop; let's get clos - er.
        Gm                      F#m|                          Bm |
           Friday was medio - cre.    Monday, I'm self-exposed, uh?
        Bm                              |                          Gm|
           Weekend party's over.    Don't stop; let's suppose - a.
        Gm                          F#m|                  Bm ||
           I won't blow your cov - er.    Opportunistic lov - er.
```

Please Don't Tell Her

Words and Music by
Jason Mraz and Eric Hinojosa

(Capo 4th fret)

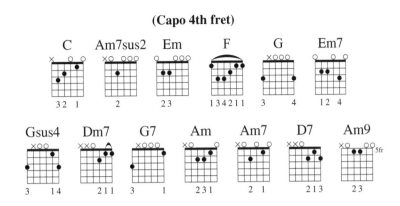

Intro   C |Am7sus2 |Em |F   G

Verse 1

‖C
I hear she's kickin' ass across the board

|Am7sus2
And rocked two hundred thousand, highest score,

|Em7
And just in time to save the world of being taken over.

|F   Gsus4 G
She's a war - rior.

|C
I couldn't play again because the game, it never ended.

|Am7sus2
Never even landed on the canon.

|Em7
Never let me in to spend my quar - ter.

|F   Gsus4 G   ‖
There's no love for me   no more.

Brtidge 1

Dm7 |G7

Say it isn't so,

             |Em |Am

How she easily come,   and she easy go.

        |Dm7 |G7

Please don't tell her that I've been meaning to miss her,

       ||

Because I don't.

Interlude 1   C |Am7 |Em7 |F   G

Verse 2

          ||C

She was the girl with the broadest shoulders.

          |Am7 |Em7

But she would die   before I crawled over them.

      |F   Gsus4 G

She is tall - er than' I am.

   |C

She knew I wouldn't mind the view there

      |Am7

Or the altitude with a mouthful of air.

Em7 |F   Gsus4   G ||

She let me down; the doubt came out until the now   became later.

Bridge 2

Dm7 |G7

Say   that it isn't so,

            |Em |Am   G

How she easily come, how she easy go.

        |F |D7

Please don't tell her 'cause she don't real - ly need to know

Chorus 1

$\parallel$**C**   **|Am7sus2**
That I'm crazy like the rest

    |Em   **|F**   **G**
Of us.

    |C   **|Am7sus2**
And I'm crazier when I'm next

    |Em   **|F**   **G** $\parallel$
To her.

Interlude 2   **C**   **|Am9**   **|Em7**   **|F**   **G**

Verse 3

$\parallel$**C**
So why after the all of everything that came and went,

    |Am7sus2   **|Em7**
I care e - nough to still be singing of the bitter end and broken eras.

    |F   **Gsus4**
I told   you I don't.

    G   **|C**
But I am only tryin' to be the best

                                |Am7sus2
With my attempt to cure the rest as - sured,

                                     |Em7
I'll aim to ease the plural hurts of the words reverse

    |F   **Gsus4**
Psychol - ogy.

Bridge 3

    G$\parallel$**Dm7**   **|G7**   **|Em**
That's   easier said,

    |Am
Easier than done.

    |Dm7   **|G7**
Please don't dare   to tell her what I've become.

    |Em7   **|Am**   **G**
Please don't mention   all the at - tention I have drawn.

    |F   **|D7**   **|**
Please don't bother,   'cause she'll feel guilty when I'm gone.

Chorus 2

           ‖**C** |**Am7sus2**

Because I'm crazy like the rest

     |**Em** |**F**   **G**

Of us.

        |**C** |**Am7sus2**

But I'm crazier when I'm next

       |**Em** |**F**   **G**

To her.

          |**C** |**Am7sus2** |**Em** |**F**   **G**

And it's so a‑mazing how she's so   self-assured.

     |**C** |**Am7sus2**

But I know she'd hate me if she knew my words.

    |**Em**

Do I hurt anymore?

   |**F**   **G** |**C** |**Am**

Do I hurt? Well, I don't.

     |**Em7** |**F**   **G** |**C**   ‖

I don't.   I don't.

The Forecast

Words and Music by
Jason Mraz and Eric Hinojosa

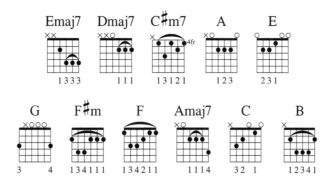

Intro Emaj7 |Dmaj7 |C#m7 |A |Emaj7 |Dmaj7 |C#m7 |A

Verse 1

‖E |A
Well, I heard that it might be raining bed sheets and lover's words.
|E |A
Let's throw out   the hotel comforter and hang the "Do   not disturb."
|E |A
Sign me up   for the storm. I'll wear my suit for the shower,
|E |A
'Cause I'll have you to keep me warm in the coldest hour.

Chorus 1

‖G   F#m |
And when the darkness falls under your hair,
F |Emaj7 |Amaj7
There I'll be.
|G |F#m   F   ‖
And crazy is the fore - cast   all week.

Interlude 1 Emaj7 |Amaj7 |Emaj7 |Amaj7

Verse 2

                    ‖**E**
Well, every kiss, every hug, is so light on the touch,
         |**A**
Deli - cate like a snowflake.
            |**E** |**A**
And I can taste, I can taste, I can taste, I can taste you all   over my face.
               |**E** |**A**
And every - one might find me foolish to not be counting on the sun.
                 |**E** |**A**
But your mouth is my umbrella now, and I'm holding your tongue.

                    ‖**G**
Chorus 2
And if the rain should pour,
         F♯m| **F** |**Emaj7** |**Amaj7**
For sure   with you I'll be,   ee.
         |**G** |**F♯m**   **F**   ‖
And crazy is the fore - cast   all week.

Interlude 2   **Emaj7** |**Amaj7** |**Emaj7** |**Amaj7** ‖

             C |**G** |
Bridge 1
             There's a good chance   in hail.
             B |**E** |
             Like cats and dogs, we'll be fly - ing.
             C |**G**
             And I'm no weather - man,
                    |**B** | ‖
But you are lightning   striking.

Bridge 2

```
      Emaj7        |Dmaj7     |C♯m7      |A
               La,  la,       la.
                             |Emaj7              |Dmaj7
      Here comes the sun        and the rain.
                       |C♯m7              |A           ||
      All at once        now they sing.
```

Verse 3

```
      E                                      |A                    |
          In the mist of the morning, pull up a blanket of a cloud
      E                                        |A
          And we'll wait for the warning of an - other come down,
               |E                      |A              |
      Because     the water is healthy for the roses in your cheeks.
      E                            |A
          My well holds plenty for penny wishing in your deep end.
```

Chorus 3

```
                        ||G
      And when the lights go out,
          F♯m  |      F          |Emaj7     |Amaj7
      No doubt,  with you I'll be.
           |G              |F♯m     F        |Emaj7        |Amaj7
      Yeah, crazy is the fore - cast   all week.
                 |G
      And if the rains should pour,
          F♯m|      F         |Emaj7     |Amaj7
      For sure   with you I'll be.
           |G              |F♯m F |Emaj7        |Amaj7        |
      Because crazy is the fore - cast     all week      long.
      G              |F♯m F    |         ||
      Crazy is the fore - cast.
```

Song for a Friend

Words and Music by
Jason Mraz, Eric Hinojosa, Dennis Morris and Dan Wilson

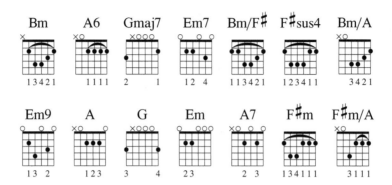

Intro

| Bm | | A6 | | Gmaj7 | | Em7 | Bm/F♯ | |
| Bm | | A6 | | Gmaj7 | | Em7 | F♯sus4 | |

Verse 1

Bm |Bm/A

"Well, you're magic," he said, but don't let it all go to your head,

|Gmaj7

'Cause I bet if you all had it all figured out,

|Em7   F♯sus4

Then you'd never get out of bed.

|Bm |Bm/A

Well, no doubt of all the thing's that I've read, what he wrote me,

|Gmaj7 |Em7

Is now sounding like the man I was hoping to be. I keep keeping it real,

Bm/F♯ |Em9

'Cause it keeps getting easier, he'll see.

|A

He's the reason that I'm laugh - ing,

|Bm A |G |

Even if there's no one else.

Em |A7 |Bm |A6 |G |Em7 F♯m

He said, you've got to love yourself.

Verse 2

               ‖**Bm**
He said, you shouldn't mum - ble when you speak,
              |**Bm/A**
But keep your tongue   up in your cheek.
         |**Gmaj7**
And if you stumble onto something to better,
          |**Em7**   **F♯m**
Remember that it's humble that you seek.
        |**Bm** |**Bm/A**
You got all   the skill you need; individ - uality.
          |**G**
You've got some - thing; call it gumption,
    |**Em7**   **F♯m**
Call it anything you want.

Bridge 1

         ‖**Em7** |**A**
Because when you play the fool now,
        |**Bm**   **A** |**Gmaj7** |
You're only fooling ev - 'ryone else.
Em9 |**A** |**Bm** |**A** |
  You're learning to love   yourself.
G |**Em7**
  Yes, you are,
    F♯m |**Bm** |**A** |**G** |**Em7**   **F♯m** ‖
You're learning to … You, hoo, you, hoo.

Bridge 2

Em |**A** |
  There's no price to pay
Em |**A** |
  When you're givin' what you take.
Em |**A** |**Bm** |**A**
  That's why it's easy to thank you,   you, hoo,
   |**G** |**Em7** **F♯m**
You,
   |**Bm** |**A** |**Gmaj7** |**Em7** **F♯m** ‖
You,   you,   you.

Verse 3

```
         Bm                                              |A
         Let's say take a break from our day and get back to the old garage,
            |G                               |Em7           F♯m
Because life's too short anyway, but at least it's better than aver - age.
            |Bm
As long as you got me and I got you,
                       |A
You know we got a lot to go around.
              |G
I'll be your    friend, your other brother,
       |Em7                  F♯m            ||
Another love to calm and com - fort you.
```


Bridge 3

```
Em7                     |A
    And I'll keep remind - ing
               |Bm       A   |Gmaj7       |
If it's the on - ly thing I ever do.
Em7          |A       |Bm      |A       |Gmaj7    |Em7 F♯m
  I will always love      you,
     |Bm        |A         |Gmaj7   |Em7 F♯m |
You,      you,        you.
Bm         |A         |Gmaj7   |Em7 F♯m      ||
```


Bridge 4

```
         Bm              |A
         It's true our love    is true.
                 |G                          |Em7       F♯m
It's you I love,    it's you I love, it's you, it's you    I love.
                    |Bm                           |A
It's true our love    is true, our love is true. It's you    I love.
                 |G                          |Em7     F♯m          ||
It's you I love,    it's you I love, it's you, it's you    I love    you, I do.
```

Interlude   Bm |F♯m/A |Gmaj7 |Em   F♯m |

                Bm |F♯m/A |Gmaj7 |Em   ‖

Chorus 1

Bm |A
Climb up over the top. Sur - vey the state of the soul.
          |Gmaj7 |Em7   F♯m |
You've got to find out for yourself whether or not you're tru - ly trying.
Bm |A
Why not give it a shot? Shake it; take control,
      |Gmaj7
Inevitably wind up finding for yourself
          |Em7   F♯m   ‖
All the strengths   you have inside   still rising.

Repeat Chorus 1 (2x)

Chorus 2

Bm |A
Climb up over the top. Sur - vey the state of the soul.
          |Gmaj7 |Em7   F♯m |
You've got to find out for yourself whether or not you're tru - ly trying.
Bm |A
Why not give it a shot? Shake it; take control,
      |Gmaj7
And inevitably wind up and find out for yourself
          |Em7   F♯m |Bm   ‖
All the strengths that you have   inside of you.

Make It Mine

Words and Music by
Jason Mraz

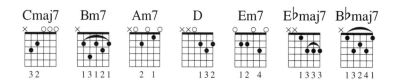

Intro   **Cmaj7** | | | |

Verse 1

|**Cmaj7** ||**Bm7**
Wake   up, everyone.

|**Bm7** |**Am7**
How   can you sleep at a time   like this?

|**Am7** |**Cmaj7**
Unless the dreamer is the real you.

|**Cmaj7** |**Bm7**
Lis - ten to your voice,

|**Bm7** |**Am7** |
The one   that tells you to taste   past the tip of your tongue.

|**Cmaj7** |
Leap and the net   will appear.

Chorus 1

||**Am7**   **D** |
I don't wanna wake   be - fore

Bm7 | **Em7**|
The dream   is o - ver.

Am7 | **D** |
I'm gonna make   it mine.

Bm7 | **Em7** |
Yes, I,   I know it.

Am7 | **D** |
I'm gonna make   it mine.

|**Cmaj7** | | | |
Yes, I'll make it all mine.

Verse 2

```
        |Cmaj7                    ||Bm7
I keep my life on a heavy ro - tation,
     |Bm7                        |Am7              |
Re - questing that it's lifting you up,    up, up and away
              |Cmaj7              |D        |Cmaj7
And over to a table at the Gratitude Cafe.
      |Cmaj7                |Bm7
And I      am finally there.
          |Bm7
And all the angels, they'll be singing,
      |Am7          |        |Cmaj7          |D        |
Ah, I,    la la la, I,   la la la, I,      la la la la, love  this.
```

Chorus 2

```
                              ||Am7      D   |
Well, I don't wanna break      be - fore
      Bm7|      Em7 |
The tour    is o - ver.
          Am7 |      D      |
I'm gonna make   it mine.
      Bm7 |        Em7 |
Yes, I,      I will own  it.
          Am7 |      D      |
I'm gonna make   it mine.
          |Cmaj7            |              |          Em7  D Am7 ||
Yes, I'll make it all mine.
```

Interlude

```
Am7      D|      Bm7|      Em7|      Am7|

Am7      D|      Bm7|      Em7|      Am7|

Am7      D|            |Cmaj7        |          |          |          ||
```

Bridge

| E♭maj7 | | |B♭maj7 |

Tim - ing's everything,

|B♭maj7 |E♭maj7

And this time there's plenty.

|E♭maj7 |B♭maj7

I   am balancing,

|B♭maj7

Care - ful and steady,

|Am7 | |D |

And reveling in energy that everyone's emit - ting.

Outro

‖Am7   D |

Well, I don't wanna wait   no more.

Bm7| Em7 |

Oh, I   wanna celebrate the whole   world.

Am7 | D |

I'm gonna make   it mine.

Bm7 | Em7|

Oh, yes, I'm following your joy.

Am7 | D |

I'm gonna make   it mine.

Bm7| Em7|

Because I,   I am o - pen.

Am7 | D |

I'm gonna make   it mine;

Bm7 | Em7 |

That's why   I will show it.

Am7 | D | Bm7|

I'm gonna make it all mine.   Gonna make,

Gonna make, gonna make,

Em7 | Am7 | D |

Gonna make it, make it, make it mine,   all mine.

|Cmaj7 | ‖

Yes, I'll make it all mine.

I'm Yours

Words and Music by
Jason Mraz

(Capo 2nd fret)

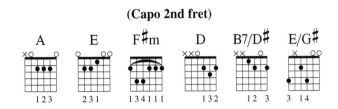

Intro   A |E |F♯m |D

Verse 1
          ‖A
Well, you done done me in; you bet I felt it.
     |E
I tried to be chill, but you're so hot that I melted.
     |F♯m |D
I fell right through the cracks. Now I'm trying to get back.
               |A
Before the cool done run out, I'll be giving it my bestest,
          |E
And nothing's going to stop me but divine intervention.
     |F♯m |D
I reckon it's again my turn to win some or learn some.

Chorus 1
          ‖A |E |F♯m
But I won't hesi - tate no more, no more.
          |D   A
It cannot wait. I'm yours.
          |E |F♯m |D   ‖
Mm,   mm, hmm, mm.

Verse 2

A |E
　　　Well, open up your mind and see like me.
                                             |F♯m
Open up your plans and, damn, you're free.
                                   |D |
Look into your heart and you'll find love, love, love, love.
A |E
Listen to the music of the moment; people dance and　　sing.
                           |F♯m
We're just one big family.
                                      |D |B7/D♯
And it's our god-forsaken right to be loved,　　loved, loved, loved, loved.

Chorus 2

　‖A　　　　|E　　　　|F♯m
So, I won't hesi - tate no more, no more.
　　　　|D
It cannot wait. I'm sure.
　　　　|A　　　　|E
There's no need to compli - cate.
　　　　|F♯m
Our time is short.
　　　|D　　　　　　　‖
This is our fate. I'm yours.

Interlude

A　　E/G♯　|F♯m　E
Scat sing...
                                   |D |B7/D♯ |
Skooch on over closer, dear,　　and I will nibble your ear.　　*Scat sing...*
A　　E/G♯　|F♯m　E　|D　　　　|B7/D♯

Verse 3

|| **A**
I've been spending way too long checking my tongue in the mirror
| **E**
And bending over backwards just to try to see it clearer.
| **F♯m** | **D**
But my breath fogged up the glass, and so I drew a new face and I laughed.
| **A**
I guess what I'll be saying is there ain't no better reason
| **E**
To rid yourself of vanities and just go with the seasons.
| **F♯m** | **D**
It's   what we aim to do. Our name is our virtue.

Chorus 3

|| **A** | **E** | **F♯m**
But I won't hesi-tate no more, no more.
        | **D** |
It cannot wait. I'm yours.
A | **E**
Open up your mind and see like me.
                                        | **F♯m**
Open up your plans and, damn, you're free.
                                | **D**
Look into your heart and you'll find that   the sky is yours.
    | **A**
So please don't, please don't, please don't…
        | **E** | **F♯m**
There's no need to complicate 'cause our time   is short.
                                | **D** | **B7/D♯** ||
This is, this is, this is our fate. I'm yours.

Outro   **A** | **E** | **F♯m** | **D** | **A** ||

Scat sing...

Lucky

Words and Music by
Jason Mraz, Colbie Caillat and Timothy Fagan

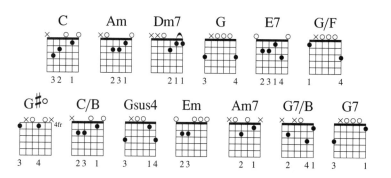

Intro   **C**

Verse 1

‖**C** |**Am**
Do you hear me talking to you?
     |**Dm7** |**G** |**E7**
Across the water, across the deep blue ocean,
     |**Am**
Under the open sky.
    |**Dm7** |**G**
Oh, my,   baby, I'm try - ing.

Verse 2

‖**C** |**Am**
Boy, I hear you in my dreams.
    |**Dm7** |**G**   **G/F**
I feel your whisper across the sea.
   |**E7** |**Am**
I keep you with me in my heart.
     |**Dm7** |**G**   **G#°**   ‖
You make it easier when life gets hard.

Chorus 1

Am |Dm7 |G
      Lucky I'm in   love with my best friend,

             |C   C/B |Am
Lucky to have been where I have been.

          |Dm7 |Gsus4 |G |
Lucky to be coming home a - gain.

C |Am |Em |G ||
Oo,   oo.

Bridge

Dm7 |Am7 |G
They don't know how long it takes,

         |Dm7 |
Waiting for a love like this.

Dm7 |Am7 |
Every time we say goodbye,

G |Dm7
  I wish we had one more kiss.

 |Dm7 |Am7 |G Am7 |G7/B ||
I'll wait for you, I promise you I will.   I'm

Chorus 2

Am7 |Dm7 |G7
     Lucky I'm in   love with my best friend,

            |C   C/B |Am7
Lucky to have been where I have been.

          |Dm7 |Gsus4 |G |
Lucky to be coming home a - gain.

Am7 |Dm7 |G7
    Lucky we're in   love in every way,

           |C   C/B |Am7
Lucky to have stayed where we have stayed.

         |Dm7 |Gsus4 |G
Lucky to be coming home some - day.

Verse 3

      ‖**C** |**Am**
And so I'm sailing through the sea
    |**Dm7** |**G**
To an island where we'll meet.
      |**E7** |**Am**
You'll hear the music fill the air.
    |**Dm7** |**G**
I'll put a flower in your hair.

Verse 4

      ‖**C** |**Am**
Though the breezes through the trees
     |**Dm7** |**G** **G/F**
Move so pretty, you're all I see.
    |**E7** |**Am**
As the world keeps spinning 'round,
   |**Dm7** |**G**   **G♯○** ‖
You hold me right here, right now.

Repeat Chorus 2

Outro

  C |**Am** |**Em** |**G** |
  Oo,   oo.
  C |**Am** |**Em** |**G** |**C** ‖
  Oo,   oo.

Butterfly

Words and Music by
Jason Mraz

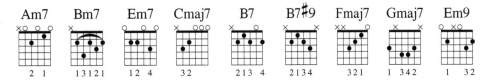

(Capo 1st fret)

Am7   Bm7   Em7   Cmaj7   B7   B7♯9   Fmaj7   Gmaj7   Em9

Intro

Am7 **Bm7** **Em7**| |**Am7** **Bm7** **Em7**| |

Am7 **Bm7** | ‖

Verse 1

Em7 | |**Am7**
    I'm taking a moment, just imag - ining that I'm dancing with you.
       |**Am7** |**Bm7**
I'm your pole and all you're wearing is your shoes.
       |**Bm7** |**Cmaj7**
You got soul; you know what to do to turn   me on
        |**B7** |
Until I write a song   about you.
Em7 | |**Am7**
    And you have your own engaging style.
       |**Am7** |**Bm7**
And you've got the knack to vivify.
       |**Bm7**
And you make my slacks a little tight;
       |**Cmaj7**
You may unfast - en them if you like.
       |**B7♯9**
That's if you crash and spend the night.

Chorus 1

```
          ‖Am7            Bm7            Em7|
```
But you don't fold, you don't fade, you got ev - 'rything you need,
```
              |Am7 Bm7               Em7 |
```
Especially me.   Sister, you've got it all.
```
                   |Am7           Bm7
```
You make the call   to make my day.
```
              |Em7
```
In your mes - sage say my name.
```
              |Am7          Bm7                    |Em7        |Am7  Bm7        |
```
Your talk is all the talk. Sister, you've got it all.
```
Em7                        |Am7  Bm7     |Em7            |
```
   You've got it all.

Verse 2

```
                        ‖Am7                        |
```
Curl your upper lip   up and let me look around.
```
Bm7                              |Em7                        |
```
   Ride your tongue along your bot - tom lip and bite down.
```
Cmaj7                                |Fmaj7
```
   And bend your back and ask those hips if I can touch.
```
                 |B7                        |
```
'Cause they're the perfect jumping off point, getting closer

Pre-Chorus 1

```
                   ‖Em7            |Am7
```
To your butter - fly. You float on by.
```
     |Bm7               |Em7
```
Oh, kiss me with your eyelashes   tonight.
```
     |Cmaj7             |Fmaj7
```
Or Eskimo your nose real close   to mine.
```
        |B7                        |
```
And let's mood the lights and finally make it right.

Chorus 2

```
            ‖Am7           Bm7          Em7 ‖
```
But you don't fold, you don't fade, you got ev - 'rything you need,
```
               |Am7 Bm7            Em7 |
```
Especially me.   Sister, you've got it all.
```
                     |Am7          Bm7
```
You make the call   to make my day.
```
                  |Em7
```
In your mes - sage say my name.
```
                  |Am7          Bm7              |Em7
```
Your talk is all the talk. Sister, you've got it all.
```
                     |Am7          Bm7         |Em7
```
You've got it all,   you've got it all, you've got it all.
```
                     |Am7          Bm7         |Em7
```
You've got it all,   you've got it all, you've got it all.
```
                     |Am7       Bm7          |
```
You've got it all.
```
Em7              |Am7        Bm7      |Em7        |            ‖
```
      You've got it a - a - ll.

Bridge

```
Am7                  |                  |Cmaj7            |
```
Doll, I need to see you pull your knee socks up.
```
Cmaj7        |Gmaj7          |                  |B7
```
Let me feel you upside down, slide in, slide out, slide over here.
```
        |B7                        ‖
```
Climb   into my mouth now, child.

Interlude

```
Em7 Am7    |Bm7 Em7    |Cmaj7 Fmaj7   |B7              |
```
Scat sing...
```
Em7 Am7    |Bm7 Em7    |Cmaj7 Fmaj7   |B7
```

Pre-Chorus 2

‖ **Em7** | **Am7**
Butter - fly, well, you landed on   my mind.

| **Bm7** | **Em7**
Damn right you landed on my ear and then you crawled   inside.

| **Cmaj7** | **Fmaj7**
And now   I see you perfectly behind   closed eyes.

| **B7** |
I want to fly with you. And I don't want to lie to you.

Chorus 3

‖ **Am7**   **Bm7**
'Cause I, 'cause I can't recall   a better day,

| **Em7**
Sun coming to shine   on the occasion.

| **Am7**   **Bm7** | **Em7**
You're an o - pen-minded lady; you've got it all.

| **Am7**   **Bm7** | **Em7**
And I never forget a face, 'cept maybe my own.

| **Am7**   **Bm7** | **Em7**
I have my days. Let's face the fact   here, it's you who's got it all.

| **Am7**   **Bm7**
You know that for - tune favors the brave.

| **Em7**
Well, let me get paid while I make you breakfast.

| **Am7**   **Bm7** | **Em7**
The rest   is up to you.   You make the call.

| **Am7**   **Bm7**
You make the call   to make my day.

| **Em7**
In your mes - sage say my name.

| **Am7**   **Bm7** | **Em7**
Your talk is all the talk. Sister, you've got it all.

Outro

‖**N.C.** |
I can't recall   a better day, sun coming to shine   on the occasion.
                 |
Hey, sophis - ticated lady.

| |**Am7**   **Bm7** |**Em7**
Oh,   you've got it all,   you've got it all, you've got it all.

          |**Am7**   **Bm7** |**Em7**
You've got it all,   you've got it all, you've got it all.

          |**Am7**   **Bm7** |**Em7**
You've got it all,   you've got it all, you've got it all.

          |**Am7**   **Bm7** |**Em7**
You've got it all,   you've got it all, you've got it all.

            |**Am7**   **Bm7** |
Hey! You've got it all.   Woo!

Em7 |**Am7**   **Bm7** |
   You've got, you, you've got it all.   Hey!

Em7 |**Am7**   **Bm7**
   You gots, you gots, you gots, you got it all.

   |**Em7** |**Am7**   **Bm7** |
Oh!   You've got, you've it all.   Hey!

Em7   **Bm7**|**Am7** |
   But - ter - fly,

B7♯9 |**Tacet** |**Em9**   ‖
Baby, well, you got it all.

Live High

Words and Music by
Jason Mraz

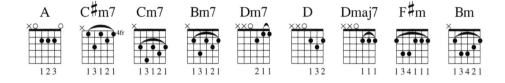

Intro   **A** |**C♯m7**   **Cm7**|**Bm7** |**Dm7**

||**A**

Verse 1   I try to picture the girl
|**C♯m7**
Through a look   -   ing glass
|**D**
And see her as a car - bon atom.
|**Dm7**
See her eyes   and stare back at them.
|**A**
See that girl
|**C♯m7**
As her own new world.
|**D** |**Dm7** |
Though a home is on the surface, she is still a universe.
A |**C♯m7**
   Glory God or Goddess peek   -   ing through the blinds.
|**D**
Are we all here standing naked,
|**Dm7** |**A**
Taking guesses at the actual date and time?
|**C♯m7**
Oh my! Justify   -   ing reasons why
|**D** |**Dm7**
Is an ab - solutely insane resolu - tion to live by.

Chorus 1

‖**A**
Live high.

|**C♯m7**
Live might - y.

Cm7 |**Bm7** |
Live righteously.

Dm7
   Taking it easy.

|**A**
Live high.

|**C♯m7**
Live might - y.

Cm7 |**Bm7** |**Dm7**
Live righteously.

Verse 2

‖**A**
And try to picture the man

|**C♯m7** |**D**
To always have an open hand and see him as a giv - ing tree.

|**Dm7** |**A**
See him as mat - ter. Matter of fact, he's not a beast.

|**C♯m7** |**D**
No, not the dev - il either. Always a good deed doer.

|**Dm7** |**A**
And it's laughter that we're making after all.

|**C♯m7**
The Call of the Wild is still an or - der nationwide.

|**D** |**Dm7** |
In the or - der of the primates, all our pol - itics are too late.

A |**C♯m7**
   Oh my, the congrega - tion in my mind

|**D** |**Dm7** ‖
Is this as - sembly singing of gratitude, practicing their loving for you.

Chorus 2

      A

Live high.

        |**C♯m7**

Live might - y.

Cm7 |**Bm7** |**Dm7**

Live   righteously.   Mm.

Taking it easy.

   |**A**

Live high.

        |**C♯m7**

Live might - y.

    Cm7|**Bm7** |**Dm7**

Oh, live   righteously.

Bridge

        ‖**Dmaj7**

Sing it out.

       |**Dm7**

And just take   it easy,

  |**C♯m7** |**F♯m**

And celebrate the malleable real - ity.

   |**Bm**

You see, nothing is ever as it seems.

    |**Dm7** | ‖

Yeah, this life is but a dream.

Outro

      A   **|C♯m7**   **Cm7** **|Bm7**
Lift me up to Thee, Almight - y!

                                    |Dm7   **|A**
Raise your hands and start acknowl - edging   He.

                      |C♯m7
If you're living it right - eously,

                    Cm7   **|Bm7**   **|Dm7**
Then you're tak - ing the eas - y way.

            |A
Live high,   live high.

            |C♯m7
Live might - y, mighty, mighty.

   Cm7   **|Bm7**   **|Dm7**
Oh,   live   righteously.

                     |A
Takin' it easy, live high. (Live High!)

         |C♯m7
Live might - y. (Lift me up to Thee!)

   Cm7   **|Bm7**   **|Dm7**
Oh, live right - eously. (Living Righteously.)

                     |A
Just take… Just, just takin' it eas - y. (Live High!)

          |C♯m7
Oh, live might - y, mighty.

   Cm7   **|Bm7**   **|Dm7**
Oh,   live righteously. And sing it out.

          |A
Just take it eas - y.

            |C♯m7
I say Live High!

   Cm7 **|Bm7**   **|Dm7**   **||**
Oh! Live Righteously!   Just take it easy.

Love for a Child

Words and Music by
Jason Mraz, Martin Terefe and Sacha Skarbek

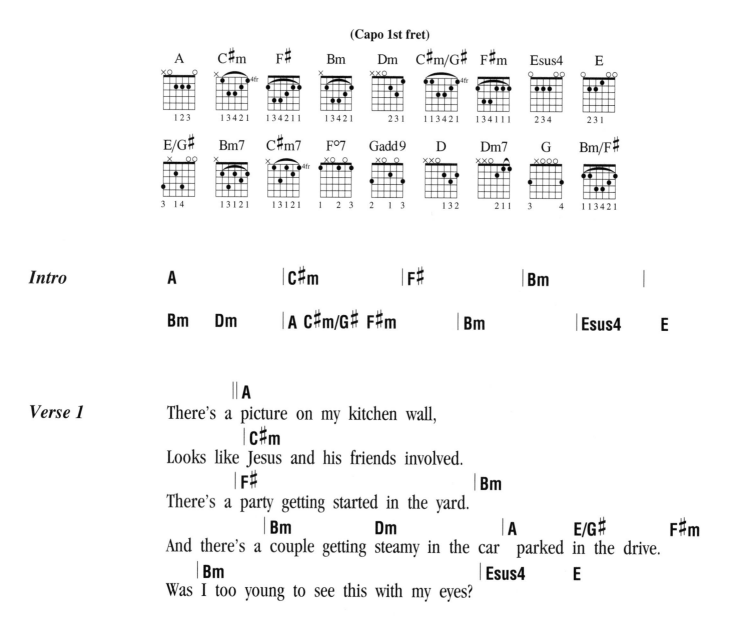

(Capo 1st fret)

Intro   A |C#m |F# |Bm |

Bm   Dm |A C#m/G# F#m |Bm |Esus4   E

Verse 1
             ‖A
There's a picture on my kitchen wall,
          |C#m
Looks like Jesus and his friends involved.
         |F# |Bm
There's a party getting started in the yard.
           |Bm   Dm |A   E/G#   F#m
And there's a couple getting steamy in the car parked in the drive.
       |Bm |Esus4   E
Was I too young to see this with my eyes?

Verse 2

       ‖ **A**
And by the pool that night, apparently
   | **C♯m**
The chemicals weren't mixed properly.
   | **F♯** | **Bm**
You hit your head and then forgot your name.
          | **Bm**   **Dm** | **A**   **E/G♯** **F♯m**
And then you woke up at the bot - tom by the drain.
          | **Bm** | **Esus4**   **E**   ‖
And now your altitude and memory's a shame.

Chorus

   A   **Bm7** | **C♯m7**   **Bm7**
  What about taking this   empty cup and filling it up
   | **A**   **Bm7**
With a little bit more of innocence.
| **C♯m7**   **Bm7**
I haven't had enough; it's probably because
       | **A**   **F°7** | **F♯m**   **Gadd9** |
When you're young, it's o - kay to be   easily ignored.
D | **Dm7** | **A**   ‖
  I'd like to believe it was all about love for a child.

Verse 3

   A | **C♯m**
  When the house was left in sham - bles,
             | **F♯** | **Bm**
Who was there to han - dle all the broken bits of glass?
    | **Bm**   **Dm** |
Was it Mom who put my dad out on his ass,
A   **E/G♯**   **F♯m**
  Or the other way a - round?
     | **Bm** | **Esus4**   **E**   ‖
Well, I'm far too old to care about that now.

Repeat Chorus

Bridge

            G   **Bm/F♯**   **|A**   **C♯m**

  It's kinda nice   to work the floor   since the divorce.

                        |G   **Bm/F♯**   **|A**

I've been enjoy‑ing both my Christmases and my birthday cakes.

     |G   **Bm/F♯**   **|A**   **C♯m**

And taking drugs and making love at far too young an age.

       |G

And they never checked to see my grades.

     |E   **|E/G♯**   **||**

What a fool I'd be to start complain - ing now.

Repeat Chorus

       |Dm7   **|A**   **||**

It was all about love.

Details in the Fabric
(Sewing Machine)

Words and Music by
Jason Mraz and Dan Wilson

(Capo 6th fret)

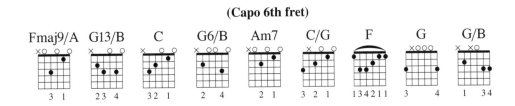

Intro

| **Fmaj9/A** | | **G13/B** | | |

| **Fmaj9/A** | | **G13/B** | |

Verse 1

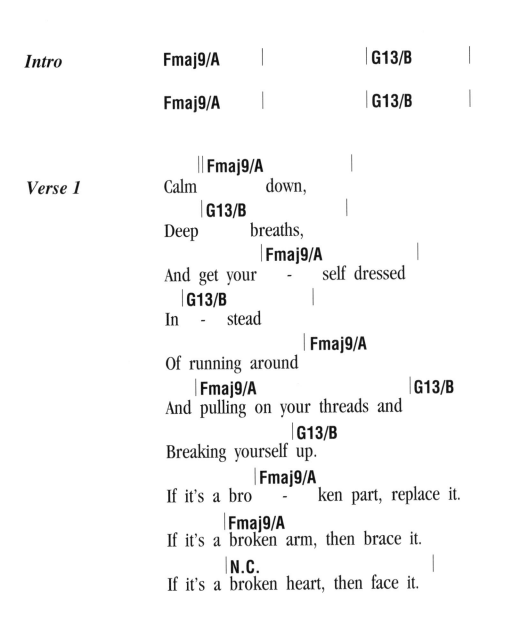

|| **Fmaj9/A** |
Calm   down,
| **G13/B** |
Deep   breaths,
| **Fmaj9/A** |
And get your   -   self dressed
| **G13/B** |
In - stead
| **Fmaj9/A**
Of running around
| **Fmaj9/A** | **G13/B**
And pulling on your threads and
| **G13/B**
Breaking yourself up.
| **Fmaj9/A**
If it's a bro   -   ken part, replace it.
| **Fmaj9/A**
If it's a broken arm, then brace it.
| **N.C.** |
If it's a broken heart, then face it.

Chorus 1

                            ‖ **C**
And hold your own,

             | **G6/B** | **Am7** |
Know your name, and go your own way.

                  | **C**
Hold your own,

            | **G6/B** | **Am7**
Know your own name, and go your own way.

 | **C/G** | **F** |
And every   -   thing

       | **G** | ‖
Will be fine.

Repeat Intro

Verse 2

             ‖ **Fmaj9/A** |
Hang   on.

               | **G13/B** |
Help is on   the way.

       | **Fmaj9/A** |
Stay   strong.

         | **G13/B** |
I'm doing   everything.

Chorus 2

                        ‖ **C**
Hold your own,

           | **G6/B** | **Am7** |
Know your name, and go your own way.

                 | **C**
Hold your own,

          | **G6/B** | **Am7**
Know your own name, and go your own way.

 | **C/G** | **F** | **G** | **F**
And every - thing, every - thing will be fine.

    | **G**
Every - thing.

Bridge

‖ C

Are the details in the fabric?

| G6/B

Are there things that make you panic?

| Am7 |

Are your thoughts results of static cling?

| C

Are there things that make you blow?

| G6/B

Hell, no reason. Go on and scream.

| Am7 | C/G | F

If you're shocked it's just the fault of faulty manufacturing.

| G | F

Every - thing will be fine.

| G | F

Every - thing in no time   at all.

| G |

Every - thing.

Chorus 3

      ‖ C

Hold your own,

      | G6/B | Am7 |

Know your name,   go your own way.

  | C

Are the details in the fabric?

  | G6/B

Are there things that make you panic?

  | Am7 |

Are your thoughts results of static cling?

  | C

Are the details in the fabric?

  | G6/B

Are there things that make you panic?

 | Am7 |

Is it Mother Nature's sewing machine?

  | C

Are there things that make you blow?

  | G6/B

Hell, no reason. Go on and scream.

  | Am7 | C/G | F

If you're shocked it's just the fault of faulty manufacturing.

  | G | F

Every - thing will be fine.

  | G | F

Every - thing in no time at all.

  | G | ‖

Hearts will hold.

Outro

| Fmaj9/A | | G13/B | |

| Fmaj9/A | | G13/B | |

| Fmaj9/A | | G/B | ‖

Coyotes

Words and Music by
Jason Mraz

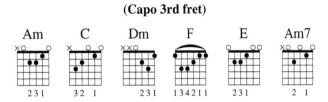

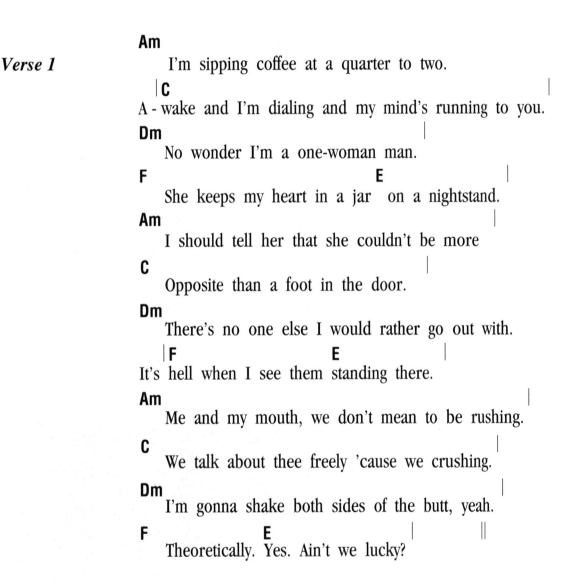

Verse 1

    Am

    I'm sipping coffee at a quarter to two.

  C

A - wake and I'm dialing and my mind's running to you.

Dm

    No wonder I'm a one-woman man.

F   **E**

    She keeps my heart in a jar on a nightstand.

Am

    I should tell her that she couldn't be more

C

    Opposite than a foot in the door.

Dm

    There's no one else I would rather go out with.

  F   **E**

It's hell when I see them standing there.

Am

    Me and my mouth, we don't mean to be rushing.

C

    We talk about thee freely 'cause we crushing.

Dm

    I'm gonna shake both sides of the butt, yeah.

F   **E**

Theoretically. Yes. Ain't we lucky?

Pre-Chorus 1

```
         Dm                                      |Am7                    |
         And when the coyotes, they sing     in the park,
         Dm                         |Am7                      |
         Is when the city life starts falling for the sea.
         Dm
         Winding roads are winding down
            |Am7                                   |
And the     flying men will hit the ground.
         Dm
         Every notion is closer to touching.
            |E                                       ||
The coyotes sing when they call on your loving.
```

Interlude 1   Am |C |Dm |F   E ||

Chorus 1

```
         Am
         We're coming back for more.
                 |C
You know why    we're coming for you.
            |Dm               |
You know we should be,
F                       E       |
   We should be togeth - er.
Am                              |C
   Cuz once we rock, we won't    wanna stop.
       |Dm                     |F          E        |
Not to - day or tomorrow. Not to - day or tomorrow,  oh, no.
Am
   You better lock your doors.
                |C
You know why,  'cause we want you.
       |Dm               |F     E       ||
Cuz we like you a lotta.
```

Interlude 2   Dm |Am |Dm |E | ||

124

Verse 2

Am |
    I wish the wild was alive like you.

C |
    I wish the wind would blow me through

Dm |
    Another opportunity to approach you,

F   **E** |
    Another telepathic rendezvous.

Am |
    I wish you well with your weapon of jargon.

C |
    You've got a double-sided lexicon.

Dm
    I gotta try to keep your attention,

  |**F**   **E** |
Gotta write using less e - moticons.

Am |
    Gotta figure out the snooze alarm.

C |
    I wanna lay in your place till dawn.

Dm
    I wanna play in the park, come on.

  |**F**   **E** | |**N.C.** ||
Now let me see your other upper echelon.

Pre-Chorus 2

Dm |**Am7** |
    And when the coyotes es - cape to New York,

Dm |**Am7** |
    Then the city life has crum - bled to the sea.

Dm |**Am7**
    And the girls will fall to the lost and found,

                    |
The flying men will hit the ground.

Dm
    Every notion is closer to touching.

  |**E** |**Am** |**C** |**Dm**
The coyotes sing when they feast on your loving.

  |**F**   **E** ||
I'm a coyote and I got a taste for your loving.

Chorus 2

Am
    We're coming back for more.
             | C
You know why   we're coming for you.
         | Dm |
You know we should be,
F   E |
    We should be togeth - er.
Am | C
    Because once we rock, we won't   wanna stop.
     | Dm | F   E |
Not to - day or tomorrow. Not to - day or tomorrow, oh, no.
Am | C
    Because once we rock, we won't   wanna stop.
     | Dm | F   E |
Not to - day or tomorrow. Oh,   mm.
Am
    We're coming back for more.
             | C
You know why   we're coming for you.
      | Dm |
You know we should be,
F   E |
    We should be togeth - er.
Am | C
    Cuz once we rock, we won't   wanna stop.
     | Dm | F   E | Am ||
Not to - day or tomorrow.

Only Human

Words and Music by
Jason Mraz and Sacha Skarbek

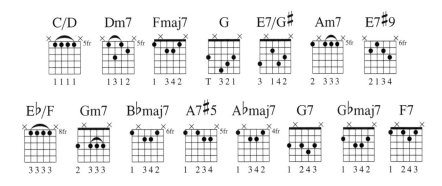

Intro   N.C. | | | ||

Verse 1

    C/D   **N.C.**

Squirrel in the tree, is he watching me?

         | |

Does he give a damn? Does he care who I am?

Dm7   **N.C.**

    I'm just a man. Is that all I am?

         |

Are my man - ners misinterpreted? Words are only human.

      |**C/D**   **N.C.** | ||

I'm hu - man.

Verse 2

C/D   **N.C**

Murderous crow, hey, what you know?

| |

What'cha rav - ing about? What'cha hold in your toes?

Dm7   **N.C.**

Is that a twig? Are you a dove of peace?

| |

Black dove undercover with another puzzle piece.

Dm7   **N.C.**

Are you a riddle to solve all along

|

Or am I over-thinking thoughts? I'm human after all,

       |**C/D**   **N.C.** | ||

Only hu - man.   Made of flesh, made of sand, made of hu - man.

Pre-Chorus

Fmaj7   **G** |

The planet's talking about a revolution.

E7/G♯   **Am7**

The natural laws ain't got   no constitution.

    |**Dm7**

They've   got a right to live their own life.

      |**E7♯9**

But we keep paving over paradise.

Chorus 1

                      ||**Dm7** |**E♭/F**

'Cause we're only hu - man.   Oh yes, we are.

      |**Gm7**

Only hu - man.

             |**B♭maj7**   **A7♯5**

If it's our only excuse,   how do you think we'll keep on

      |**Dm7** |**E♭/F**

Being only hu - man?   Oh yes, we are.

     |**Gm7** |**B♭maj7**   **A7♯5** ||

Only hu - man.   So far,   so far.

Interlude　　　　**N.C**　　　|　　　　　|**C/D**　　　　|　　　**Dm7**　　　||

　　　　　　　　　　　C/D　　　　**N.C.**

Verse 3　　　　　　Up in the major's tree,

　　　　　　　　　　　　　　　　　　|　　　　　　　　　　　　　　|

The one he planted back when he was just a boy back in 1923.

　　　　　　　　　　　C/D　　　**N.C.**

　　　　　　　　　　Thirty meters and a foot, take a look,

　　　　　　　|　　　　　　　　　　　　　　　　|

Take a climb. What you'll find is the product of a seed.

Dm7　　　　　　　　　**N.C**　　　　　　　　　　|

　　　　　　The seed is sown; all alone it grows above,　with a heart of love,

　　　　　　　　　　　　　　　　|**C/D**　　　　**N.C.**

A sharpened shelter of　　　　the ani - mals of land

　　　　　　　　　　　　　|　　　　　　　　　　　　||

And cold weather breath - ing. We're all breathing.

Repeat Pre-Chorus

Repeat Chorus 1

　　　　　　　　　　　||**B♭maj7**　　　　　**A7♯5**

Bridge　　　　And this place, it will out - live me.

　　　　　　|**A♭maj7**　　　　　　　　　**G7**

Be - fore I get to heaven I'll climb　that tree.

　　　　　　|**G♭maj7**　　　　　　　　　**F7**

And I will have to give my thanks

　　　　　　|**G♭maj7**　　　　　　　　　**A♭maj7**　　　　|**B♭maj7**

For giving me the branch to swing　　on.

　　　　　　　　　A7♯5　|**A♭maj7**　　　**G7**

If I ev - er fall　　　in love,

　　　　　　|**G♭maj7**　　　　　　　**F7**

I'll hope to get myself a ba - by.

　　　　　　|**G♭maj7**　　　　　　　　|**A♭maj7**

I will let my children have their way.

Chorus 2

       ‖Dm7 |E♭/F

Because we're only hu - man. Oh yes, we are.

   |Gm7

Only hu - man.

   |B♭maj7 A7♯5 |Dm7 |E♭/F |Gm7

So far, so far.

   |B♭maj7 A7♯5 ‖

So far, so far.

Outro   N.C C/D |N.C. Dm7 |N.C. C/D |N.C. ‖

The Dynamo of Volition

Words and Music by
Jason Mraz

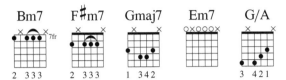

Verse 1

||**Bm7**
I got the dyna - mo of volition, the p-pole position,

|**F♯m7**   **Gmaj7**
Auto - matic transmission with 1 - low emissions.

|**Bm7** |**F♯m7**   **Gmaj7**
I'm a brand-new addition to the old edition with the love uncondition - al.

|**Bm7** |**F♯m7**
And I'm a drama abolitionist, damn, no opposition to my proposition.

Gmaj7
Half of a man, half magician.

|**Bm7**
Half a politician holding the mic like ammunition,

|**F♯m7**   **Gmaj7**
And my vision is as simple as light.

|**Bm7**
Ain't no reason we should be in a fight, no demolition.

|**F♯m7**   **Gmaj7**
Get to vote, get to say what you like, procreation.

|**Bm7** |
Compo - sitions already written by themselves.

F♯m7   **Gmaj7** |
Heck is for the people not believing in gosh.

Chorus 1

‖ **Bm7**
Good job.

‖ **F♯m7**　　　　**Gmaj7**
Get 'em up way high. Gimme, gimme that high　　five.

| **Bm7**
Good　　times.

| **F♯m7**　　　　**Gmaj7**
Get 'em way down low. Gimme, gimme that low　　dough.

| **Bm7**
Good　　God.

| **F♯m7**　　　　**Gmaj7**
Bring 'em back again. Gimme, gimme that high　　ten.

| **Bm7 Tacet**　　　　　　| **F♯m7**　　**Gmaj7**　　　　　‖
You're the best definition of good inten - tions.

Bridge 1

Em7　　　　　　　　| **F♯m7**　　　　　　　　| **Gmaj7**
　I do not answer the call if I do not know who is calling.

| **G/A**　　　　　　　　　　　　　|
I guess the whole point of it all is that we never know really.

Em7　　　　　　　　| **F♯m7**　　　　　　　　　　| **Gmaj7**
　I'm trying to keep with the Joneses while waiting for guns and the roses

| **G/A**　　　　　　　| **Bm7**　　　　　|
To finish what we all sup - pose is gonna be the shit, as - suming.

F♯m7　　**Gmaj7**　　| **Bm7**　　　　| **F♯m7**　　**Gmaj7**

Verse 2

‖**Bm7** **Tacet**　　　　　　　　　　　　　　　　　　　　　｜**F♯m7**
Oh, fists knock bumping and wrists locked twisting up a rizla.
Gmaj7　　　　　　　　　｜**Bm7**　　　　　　　　　　　｜**F♯m7**
Kid Icarus on the tran - sistor. Nintendo been giving me the blister.
Gmaj7　　　　　　　　　　｜**Bm7**
I bend over, take it in the kisser.

　　　　　　　　　　　　　　　　　　　｜**F♯m7**
My best friends are hitting on my　　　　　sister.
　Gmaj7　　　　　　　　　｜**Bm7**
I try to tell 'em that they still a wisher,
　　　　　　　　　　　　　　　｜**F♯m7**
'Cause she already got herself a mister.
　　　　Gmaj7　　　　　　　　　　　｜**Bm7**
And be - sides, that's gross, don't wanna dis her.
　　　　｜**F♯m7**　　　　**Gmaj7**　　　　　　　｜
A-d-d-d-d-d-didn't I say, didn't I say.

Chorus 2

　　　　　　　　　　　‖**Bm7**
Good job.

　　　　　　　　　　　　　｜**F♯m7**　　　　　　**Gmaj7**
Get 'em up way high. Gimme, gimme that high　　　five.
　　　｜**Bm7**
Good　　　times.
　　　　　　　　　　　　　　　｜**F♯m7**　　　　　**Gmaj7**
Get 'em way down low. Gimme, gimme that low　　　dough.
　　　｜**Bm7**
Good　　　God.
　　　　　　　　　　　　　　｜**F♯m7**　　　　　　**Gmaj7**
Bring 'em back again. Gimme, gimme that high　　　ten.
　　　｜**Bm7** **Tacet**　　　　　　　　　｜**F♯m7**　　　　**Gmaj7**　　　　‖
You're the best definition of good versus evil.

Verse 3

                        Bm7 |F♯m7
                         I do not keep up with statistics.
             Gmaj7 |Bm7
I   do not sleep without a mistress.
                        |F♯m7   Gmaj7 |Bm7
I do not eat unless it's fixed with some   kind of sweet, like a licorice.
                        |F♯m7
My home is deep inside the mystics.
             Gmaj7 |Bm7
I'm   known to keep digging on ex - istence.
                        |F♯m7
I'm holding in the heat like a fish stick.
Gmaj7
My phone, it beeps

Bridge 2

                        ‖Em7
Because I missed it.
                        |F♯m7 |Gmaj7
I do not answer the call if I do not know who is calling.
                        |G/A |
I'm making no sense of it all. Say, can I get a witness?
Em7 |F♯m7 |Gmaj7
     I'm only a boy in a   story, just a hallucina - tory
                        |G/A |
Tripping on nothing there is, living in the wilderness.
Em7 |F♯m7 |Gmaj7
     With a tiger spot on my   back, living life of a   cat.
                        |G/A |
I just want to relax   here and write another rap tune.
Em7 |F♯m7 |Gmaj7
     Driving off on your blind man's bike, you can say just what you like;
     |G/A |Bm7 |F♯m7   Gmaj7 |
Oh, nothing can stop you.

Bm7 |F♯m7   Gmaj7

134

Chorus 3

‖ **Bm7**
Good job.

|**F♯m7**　　　　**Gmaj7**
Get 'em up way high. Gimme, gimme that high　　five.

|**Bm7**
Good　　times.

|**F♯m7**　　　　**Gmaj7**
Get 'em way down low. Gimme, gimme that low　　dough.

|**Bm7**
Good　　God.

|**F♯m7**　　　　**Gmaj7**
Bring 'em back again. Gimme, gimme that high　　ten.

|**Bm7 Tacet**
You're the best, you're the best, you're the best, you're the best,

|**F♯m7**　　　　**Gmaj7**
You're the best, you're the best, you're the best.

Chorus 4

‖ **Bm7**
Good job.

|**F♯m7**　　　　**Gmaj7**
Get 'em up way high. Gimme, gimme that high　　five.

|**Bm7**
Good　　times.

|**F♯m7**　　　　**Gmaj7**
Get 'em way down low. Gimme, gimme that low　　dough.

|**Bm7**
Good　　God.

|**F♯m7**　　　　**Gmaj7**
Bring 'em back again. Gimme, gimme that high　　ten.

|**Bm7 Tacet**　　　　　　|**F♯m7**　　　　**Gmaj7**
You're the best definition of good inten - tions.

|**Bm7 Tacet**　　　　　　|**F♯m7**　　　　**Gmaj7**
You're the best definition of good inten - tions.

|**Bm7 Tacet**　　　　　　|**F♯m7**　　　　**Gmaj7**
You're the best definition of good inten - tions.

|**Tacet Bm7**　　　　　　|**F♯m7**　　　　**Gmaj7**　　　‖
You're the best　　　　around.

If It Kills Me

Words and Music by
Jason Mraz, Martin Terefe and Sacha Skarbek

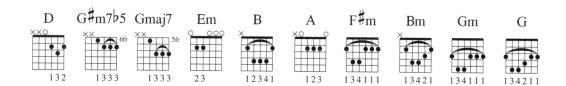

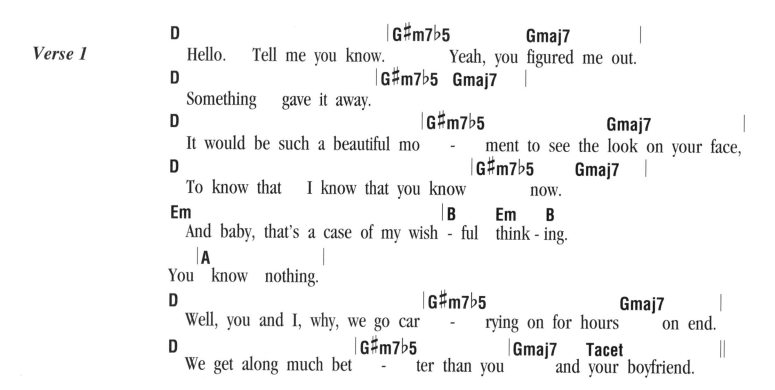

Verse 1

```
  D                              |G♯m7♭5          Gmaj7            |
  Hello.   Tell me you know.        Yeah, you figured me out.
  D                              |G♯m7♭5  Gmaj7   |
  Something    gave it away.
  D                              |G♯m7♭5            Gmaj7           |
  It would be such a beautiful mo    -    ment to see the look on your face,
  D                              |G♯m7♭5          Gmaj7   |
  To know that   I know that you know        now.
  Em                             |B      Em     B
  And baby, that's a case of my wish - ful  think - ing.
       |A                  |
  You  know  nothing.
  D                              |G♯m7♭5                Gmaj7        |
  Well, you and I, why, we go car    -    rying on for hours     on end.
  D                      |G♯m7♭5      |Gmaj7    Tacet          ||
  We get along much bet    -   ter than you        and your boyfriend.
```

Chorus 1

D |F#m
Well, all I really want do is love   you.
                         |Bm
A kind much closer than friends   use,
                         |Gm |
But I still can't say it after all   we've been through.
D |F#m
And all I really want from you is to feel   me
                         |Bm
As the feeling inside keeps build - ing.

                         |Gm |
And I will find a way to you if it kills   me, if it kills me.
D |Gm ||

Verse 2

D |G#m7♭5   Gmaj7 |
How long   can I go on   like this,   wishing to kiss you
D |G#m7♭5 Gmaj7 |
Before I   rightly explode?
D |G#m7♭5
Well, this double life I lead isn't health - y for me;
        Gmaj7 |
In fact, it makes me nervous.
D |G#m7♭5 Gmaj7 |
If I get caught I could be risking it all.
Em |B Em B |A ||
'Cause maybe there's a lot that I miss in case I'm wrong.

D |F♯m
All I really want do is love   you.
                             |Bm
A kind much closer than friends   use,
                        |Gm |
But I still can't say it after all   we've been through.
D |F♯m
And all I really want from you is to feel   me
                         |Bm
As the feeling inside keeps build - ing.
                             |Gm
And I will find a way to you if it kills   me, if it kills me,
        |D |Gm ||
If it kills me, ah.

Em
If I should be so bold,
 |B   Em
I'd ask you to hold my heart   in your hand;
 |B   Em B |A
I'd tell you from the start how I've longed to be your man.
    |A   Tacet |
But I never said a word. I guess I've gone and missed my chance again.
D |F♯m |G |Gm ||

Chorus 3

    D |F♯m
Well, all I really want do is love   you.
                         |Bm
A kind much closer than friends   use,
                    |Gm |
But I still can't say it after all   we've been through.
D |F♯m
  And all I really want from you is to feel   me
                    |Bm
As the feeling inside keeps build - ing.
                        |Gm
And I will find a way to you if it kills   me, if it kills me,
     |D |F♯m
If it kills me.
               |Bm |Gm |
Oh, I think it might kill me.
D |F♯m
  And all I really want to do is to feel   you.
                        |B
Yeah, the feeling inside keeps build - ing.
                    |Gm
I'll find a way to you if it kills   me, if it kills me.
     |D |Gm |D ||
It might kill me.

A Beautiful Mess

Words and Music by
Jason Mraz, Mona Tavakoli, Chaska Potter, Mai Bloomfield and Becky Gebhard

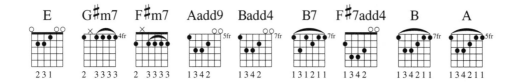

Intro

E |G♯m7 |F♯m7 |Aadd9   Badd4 |

E |G♯m7 |F♯m7 |Aadd9   Badd4

Verse 1

‖**E** |

You've got the best of both worlds;

G♯m7 |**F♯m7**

    You're the kind of girl who can take down a man

|**Aadd9**   **Badd4**

And lift him back up a - gain.

|**E** |

You are   strong but you're needy.

G♯m7

Humble but you're greedy,

|**F♯m7** |**Aadd9**   **Badd4**

And based on your body language and shoddy cursive I've been read - ing,

|**E**

Your style is quite selective,

|**G♯m7**

Though your mind is rather reckless.

|**F♯m7** |**Aadd9**   **Badd4**   ‖

Well, I guess it just suggests that this is just what happi - ness is.

Pre-Chorus 1

Aadd9 | |Badd4 | |
And what a beautiful mess this is.

Aadd9 | |Badd4 B7 |
It's like we're picking up trash in   dresses.

Chorus 1

‖E |G♯m7 |
Well, it   kind of hurts when the   kind of words you write

F♯m7 |Aadd9   Badd4
Kind of turn them - selves into knives.

        |E |G♯m7
And don't mind my nerve. You could   call it fiction,

  |F♯m7 |Aadd9 Badd4 |F♯7add4
But I   like being submerged in your contradic - tions, dear.

   |Aadd9 |F♯7add4 |
'Cause here   we are,

Aadd9 |E |G♯m7 |F♯m7 |Aadd9 B
Here   we   are.

Verse 2

‖E |G♯m7
Although   you were biased, I love your advice.

 |F♯m7
Your comebacks, they're quick

         |Aadd9   Badd4
And probably have to do with your inse - curities.

     |E
There's no   shame in being crazy,

 |G♯m7 |
De - pending on how you take these

F♯m7 |Aadd9   Badd4   ‖
Words I'm paraphrasing, this re - lationship we're   staging.

Pre-Chorus 2

Aadd9 | **|Badd4** | |
And what a beautiful mess this is.

Aadd9 | **|Badd4 B7** |
It's like picking up trash in   dresses.

Chorus 2

||E **|G♯m7** |
Well, it   kind of hurts when the   kind of words you say

F♯m7 **|Aadd9** **Badd4** |
Kind of turn them - selves into blades.

E **|G♯m7**
Kind and courteous is   a life I've heard,

|F♯m7 **|Aadd9** **Badd4** **|F♯7add4**
But it's   nice to say that we played in the dirt,   oh dear.

|Aadd9 **|F♯7add4**
'Cause here   we are,

|Aadd9 ||
Here we are.

Bridge

E **|G♯m7** |
(Here we are.)   Here we are.

F♯m7 **|Aadd9** **Badd4** |
Here we are.   Here we are.

E **|G♯m7** |
(Here we are.   Here we are.)

F♯m7 **|Aadd9** **Badd4** ||
Here we are.   We're still here.

Pre-Chorus 3

```
Aadd9                    |              |Badd4        |           |
         And what a beautiful mess this is.
Aadd9           |                        |B                      |
         It's like    taking a guess when the only answer is yes.
```

Chorus 3

```
            ‖E                    |G♯m7
Through    timeless words and        priceless pictures
     |F♯m7              |Aadd9       Badd4
We'll    fly like birds        not of this earth.
       |E                      |G♯m7
And    tides they turn, and        hearts disfigure,
         |F♯m7                      |Aadd9        Badd4
But that's       no concern when we're wounded togeth - er.
         |E                  |G♯m7
And we    tore our dresses and        stained our shirts,
     |F♯m7                    |
But it's      nice today.
     |A           B          |           ‖
Oh, the wait was so worth it.
```

Outro

```
        E              |G♯m7        |F♯m7         |Aadd4  Badd4 |E        ‖
```

   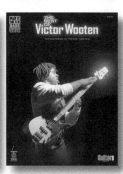